Relaxation Techniqu

I dedicate this book to my special and gentle mother, Margaret Cunningham McKie (née Patrick), and my quiet and unassuming father-in-law, James McLean Muir, both of whom died suddenly, aged 85, while I was writing this book. I owe so much to them both, and my world will never be quite the same again.

Relaxation Techniques
Alice Muir

For UK order enquiries: please contact Bookpoint Ltd,
130 Milton Park, Abingdon, Oxon OX14 4SB.
Telephone: +44 (0) 1235 827720. Fax: +44 (0) 1235 400454.
Lines are open 09.00–17.00, Monday to Saturday, with a 24-hour
message answering service. Details about our titles and how to
order are available at www.teachyourself.com

For USA order enquiries: please contact McGraw-Hill Customer
Services, PO Box 545, Blacklick, OH 43004-0545, USA.
Telephone: 1-800-722-4726. Fax: 1-614-755-5645.

For Canada order enquiries: please contact McGraw-Hill
Ryerson Ltd, 300 Water St, Whitby, Ontario L1N 9B6, Canada.
Telephone: 905 430 5000. Fax: 905 430 5020.

Long renowned as the authoritative source for self-guided
learning – with more than 50 million copies sold worldwide –
the **Teach Yourself** series includes over 500 titles in the fields of
languages, crafts, hobbies, business, computing and education.

British Library Cataloguing in Publication Data: a catalogue record
for this title is available from the British Library.

Library of Congress Catalog Card Number: on file.

First published in UK 2009 by Hodder Education, part of
Hachette UK, 338 Euston Road, London NW1 3BH.

First published in US 2009 by The McGraw-Hill Companies, Inc.

This edition published 2010.

Previously published as *Teach Yourself Relaxation*.

The **Teach Yourself** name is a registered trade mark of
Hodder Headline.

Typeset by MPS Limited, A Macmillan Company.

Printed in Great Britain for Hodder Education, an Hachette UK
Company, 338 Euston Road, London NW1 3BH, by CPI Cox &
Wyman, Reading, Berkshire RG1 8EX.

The publisher has used its best endeavours to ensure that the URLs
for external websites referred to in this book are correct and active
at the time of going to press. However, the publisher and the
author have no responsibility for the websites and can make no
guarantee that a site will remain live or that the content will remain
relevant, decent or appropriate.

Hachette UK's policy is to use papers that are natural, renewable
and recyclable products and made from wood grown in sustainable
forests. The logging and manufacturing processes are expected to
conform to the environmental regulations of the country of origin.

Impression number   10 9 8 7 6 5 4 3 2 1
Year   2014 2013 2012 2011 2010

Acknowledgements

Over the past 25 years, there are so many people who have contributed to my thinking and to my practice of relaxation, not least my family. Some, sadly, are no longer with us. Thank you all for your inspiration, and for your support: Sheila Crichton, Frances Elder, Jean McGowan, Prof. Kevin Power, Dr David Lewis, Jean Chapman, Margaret McLean, Dr Kenneth Hambly, George Greig, Ann Burnett, Eileen Wilson, Victoria Roddam, Denise Robertson, Joe Harkins, Dr Jim White, Dorothy McGowan, Kay Hoy, Zena Wight, Dr Drew Walker, Dr Carol Davidson.

Contents

Meet the author		xi
Only got a minute?		xiv
Only got five minutes?		xvi
Only got ten minutes?		xviii
1	**Relaxation – a skill with a long history**	**1**
	Benefits of relaxation	2
	Uses of relaxation	5
	How to relax	7
	Why telling yourself to relax is difficult	9
	Relaxation techniques	11
2	**Relaxation, stress and tension explained**	**16**
	What is relaxation?	16
	The stress response	18
	Brainwaves	19
	Getting tension levels right	21
	Causes of tension	24
	What is stress?	27
	Are we more stressed today?	30
	Stress and anxiety	32
	Panic attacks	33
3	**Coping with stress and tension**	**38**
	Slow down and make time for relaxation	39
	Exercise and lifestyle	42
	Thinking style	43
	Sorting out your priorities	47
	Cushioning yourself and feeling good	49
	Work stress	52
	What about medication?	54
4	**Vulnerability to tension or stress**	**59**
	Hot spots	60
	Personality	63
	Attitudes	71

	Previous experiences	71
	Ways of coping with stress	72
5	**Relaxing your body**	**77**
	Understanding helps you to relax	77
	Changes in breathing	78
	Symptoms of hyperventilation	82
	Basic relaxation prerequisites	87
	Progressive muscle relaxation	88
	Autogenic training	90
	A good night's sleep	93
	Aids to relaxation	97
6	**Relaxed body language**	**101**
	Body language	101
	Relaxation on the go	104
	Making things better	106
	Cultural differences	115
7	**A relaxed mind and calm thinking**	**117**
	How to relax the mind	118
	Relaxed thinking	120
	Thinking more positively	125
	Gaining a sense of control	127
	Thinking errors	128
	Relax your mouth and eyes	131
	Using sounds	132
	Guided imagery	135
8	**Relaxing mind and body together**	**139**
	Meditation	140
	Mindfulness	145
	Yoga	147
	T'ai chi	149
	Petting an animal	150
	Qigong	152
	Neurolinguistic programming	153
	Cognitive behavioural therapy	156
9	**More alternative and complementary therapies**	**161**
	Massage	162
	Reflexology	166

Acupuncture 168
Biofeedback 171
Alexander Technique 173
Reiki 175
Emotional Freedom Technique 177
Humour and smiling 178
10 Making the most of the Internet and modern technology 184
For beginners 185
Think before you click 186
Non-computer-based equipment 187
Podcasts on the Internet 189
Biofeedback using a computer 191
Social networking sites 193
Blogs and blogrolls 195
11 Relaxation and your feelings 200
A dual approach 200
Anger 201
Your triggers 205
Coping with your anger 206
Coping with someone else who is angry 209
Jealousy 213
Dealing with criticism and put-downs 215
Giving criticism 219
Anxiety 220
Obsessive-compulsive disorder 223
12 Relaxation in situations 228
Preparing to do anything which might make you tense 229
Coping with authority figures 231
Interview skills 232
Pointers for exams or tests 234
Giving a presentation, speech or short talk 236
13 Relaxation and your mood 241
Reasons for mood problems 242
What you can do to help yourself 246
Coping with depression 247
Dealing with low mood 248

14 What now? Relaxation as a way of life   **254**
  Motivation and persistence   254
  Visualization   257
  The big picture   258
  Personal action plan   260
  Taking it further   **264**
  Index   **272**

Meet the author

I first taught relaxation to a small community group in 1982.
This was a part of some voluntary work I was doing at that
time. I had learned the basics of this newly emerging skill at
a workshop run by a local charity. My interest in relaxation
came about because I had been finding work stressful as a
young, newly qualified teacher who had been catapulted into
a secondary school at a time of serious industrial unrest and
when the school-leaving age had just risen from 15 to 16.
I found relaxation an invaluable and immense help to me, and
was pleased to pass on what I had learned to a local group of
interested and tense individuals.

The thing about those very early days which seems so strange
now, was that GPs at that time frowned upon relaxation and
using recordings of relaxation techniques, seeing this as coming
very much from the other side of the track, or even as some
bizarre kind of 'hocus pocus'. Some of the women in my group
were told not to go back to their GPs if they were going to
persist with this dubious practice.

This story clearly shows just how much times have changed, and
how they continue to change, sometimes beyond all recognition,
and always in an unpredictable and uncontrollable fashion. And
this gives us two reasons why people may be more tense and
more 'grumpy' these days: change, and our lack of control over it.
Television has made much of 'grumpy old men' and 'grumpy
old women', which, sadly, does strike a chord with most of us,
amusing though this may be. But it doesn't matter what age
we are, change is stressful, and so is feeling we have little or no
control over these changes.

There are many other reasons why there is so much tension
around today – too many to go into here. But the speed

and complexity of life, and its highly competitive nature are foremost amongst them. The changing and unpredictable nature of personal and family relationships, and the more pressurized atmosphere of the workplace are two of the top causes of tension, with drugs, alcohol and poverty coming in third. These are just my views of course, and doubtless you'll have your own opinions, but the statistics on absence from work due to mental health problems, chief among which are stress, tension, anxiety and depression, speak for themselves and make grim reading.

From my early introduction to relaxation in the early 1980s, I was interested enough to take a degree in psychology, and to follow that up with a masters degree. This was achieved through several years of researching the best way to train practice nurses and health visitors to be able to provide on-the-spot advice to the thousands consulting their GP every year because of stress and tension. This has defined my work for the past 15 years, which has primarily involved creating and running courses on relaxation and stress, mainly for the health professionals on the front line of dealing with this immense problem.

I was therefore delighted to be asked to produce a new edition of *Teach Yourself Relaxation*, and I had no hesitation in saying yes. I have thoroughly enjoyed bringing together information and techniques from the wide array of sources now available in this fascinating world of 'hocus pocus'. This shady and 'alternative' world has now come firmly into the mainstream, and is being actively encouraged by the NHS, with many GPs themselves learning how to relax in order to cope better with their very stressful occupation.

This book is a treasure trove of numerous different approaches to relaxation for you to enjoy, learn about and try for yourself. You'll be able to look around the Aladdin's cave which is the colourful world of relaxation, and see what every corner of it has to offer. You'll find ancient methods such as meditation, yoga and t'ai chi; more recent methods like mindfulness, progressive muscle relaxation, scanning, quick relaxation, and breathing exercises; and absolutely cutting edge relaxation using biofeedback devices and specialist computer programs. There is no assumed knowledge, everything will be explained clearly, and there are abundant step-by-step and straightforward instructions for you to try out what's on offer for yourself.

There is nothing in the book that requires you to be particularly fit or active, or exert yourself particularly. In fact, the term 'relaxation exercise' is really a misnomer which has led to misunderstanding. It's better to think of relaxation techniques, or methods, rather than exercises. Nevertheless, it is always wise to check with your doctor if you feel unsure of any technique.

I've also included alternative and complementary therapies which have been shown to be effective for relaxation. Where possible, self-help techniques for these are given, but if this is not possible, vital information about consulting a therapist is included to help you if you decide to try these.

There are also sections which will give you guidance for coping with the many situations which can produce tension: an interview, driving test or exam, and giving a presentation, are just some examples. Specific know-how for these situations teamed with appropriate relaxation skills provide the ideal strategy for dealing with life's difficult situations. There are so many of these today, and we are all expected to sail through them with ease. Similar material on how to deal better with feelings like anger and jealousy are included, as well as some insights into coping with criticism and mood swings.

The book concludes with a chapter that guides you through a review of what have been the main points for you in the book, and helps you decide how to take your new skills forward, develop them further and keep them on top form. This is a book which you'll want to return to, and dip into again and again, as it has so much to offer on the wonderful art of relaxation.

I hope you will enjoy my book on 'hocus pocus'.

Only got a minute?

Relaxation – the forgotten skill

We are all born able to relax. We don't have to give it a moment's thought. It just happens. Think back to your early childhood. Do you remember feeling tense or stressed then? Most of us were relaxed and carefree as young children. But with the ever quickening pace and stress of life as we get older, we can easily fall into the tension habit, and we can actually forget how to relax. We can forget what it feels like to be relaxed. How nice it feels. And how 'normal' that feeling is.

You get so used to your shoulders and across the back of your neck being tense that you simply don't notice it. The muscles around your eyes and across your forehead jump to attention whenever you wake in the morning. Arching your back when you are driving goes unnoticed in the roar and bustle of the traffic. As the day goes on, you can clench your teeth or hold your jaw taut, or clutch the phone in a vice-like grip. All unnoticed.

It's so important to rekindle that memory of childhood, and to learn how to relax again and do what used to come naturally to us. To just 'be' relaxed, without ever having to work at it.

So, try it now for yourself. Take 20 seconds or so, just to mentally scan through your whole body looking for any tense areas. Go on, give it a go. Just mentally scan over your body. Found any tense areas? Now, simply let that tension go, and allow your whole body to relax completely. Repeat this 'complete body scan' once more, and relax any tension you find. Feel more relaxed now? Do this a couple of times each day, and you'll be amazed at how much better you feel.

5 Only got five minutes?

Every breath that you take

It may surprise you to know that the way you breathe is directly connected to how relaxed or tense you feel. A tense or stressful situation tends to make you breathe a little faster. Not noticeably, just a few extra breaths every minute. But these extra breaths are enough to make changes to the delicate balance of our bodies, upsetting the proportions of oxygen and carbon dioxide in your blood, making you feel a little jumpy or short-tempered. You can even feel light-headed, unreal, tingly, panicky or lacking in concentration. It can be hard to make decisions or to remember names and numbers, even familiar ones like your own telephone number and address. And that can be so embarrassing. And of course all of this will simply add even more to your tension.

Feeling tense also makes it more likely that you'll be breathing mainly with your upper chest, as a hand placed there for a few moments will quickly reveal. Breathing from the abdomen, or tummy area, is actually the most relaxed and effective way to breathe. Look at a sleeping baby or toddler, or a sleeping animal, and you'll see relaxed tummy breathing in action. All tummy movement and very little chest movement.

All the odd sensations brought about by breathing too fast will only make a tense situation even worse, as you feel powerless to do anything about it, and feel even less well equipped to cope with the situation. It can even make you more likely to lose your temper and be aggressive or sarcastic. You can begin to doubt your own abilities. Something of a downward spiral, which we can all fall into, without even noticing it.

To make things better, and climb back out of the spiral, you have to reverse the process which made you feel and react like this. Relaxation can put things right again with your breathing.

Try this

You can do this anytime, and it will make you feel more relaxed. You don't have to be in a tense or stressful situation to do this though. In fact, it's much the best thing to learn how to do this when you're already fairly relaxed.

Here's what to do. Take a long and gentle breath in to your own slow silent count of one, two, three, and then whenever you feel ready, gently sigh out the breath to your own slow and silent count of one, two, three.

Do this for at least four or five complete breath cycles – more if you have time.

If you can repeat this at least three times a day, you'll break into the downward spiral that over-breathing, or 'hyperventilating', can produce, and you'll find you'll gradually begin breathing more slowly, and more with your abdomen. And you'll feel much, much better too.

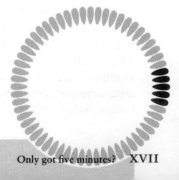

10 Only got ten minutes?

Something for everyone – the choice is yours

Being able to relax whenever you want is a most amazing skill to have. And it couldn't be easier, and more straightforward to learn. **Nothing complicated.** Nothing strenuous, energetic or difficult. You don't need a good memory, or to wear special clothing. There's no need to be very fit, though it's always a good idea to be as fit as you can be for general health reasons. You can practise and use relaxation absolutely anywhere, anytime. It needn't take up hours of your time – unless you want it to. You can learn a few basic skills in minutes, and then use these for a lifetime. Relaxing completely for just ten minutes a day can transform your life. And you can build from there, learning as much as you want, and spending as much time on it as you choose. The art of relaxation is a very broad school, with something there for everyone. Best of all it's fun, undemanding, and enjoyable to learn.

Being able to relax regularly has so many benefits too. You'll feel calmer, and more together, and you'll have a feeling of peace and contentment that you may have forgotten was possible. It's a marvellous cushion from stress, and can bring you an inner glow, as well as a feeling of being more in control of your life. The hurly burly and breakneck speed that was your life can be replaced by a slower and more predictable pace. You can have more energy, be able to concentrate, and start to plan and make decisions again. You can even pass on what you learn to those you care about, if they need to chill out more. There are no side effects and, best of all, being relaxed just feels really good. A fantastic feeling of stillness and inner harmony that's hard to describe, without experiencing it for yourself.

There are lots of ways to relax, with an almost limitless choice at your fingertips. There's no one size fits all about relaxation. Choose what suits you. Better still, choose what works best for you.

Choose a way of relaxing which brings you enjoyment and calmness, and fits in with your lifestyle. That way you'll find it will all happen without your having to try too hard. That's the very best way to learn to relax.

There are lots and lots of simple and quickly learned methods, which you can use straight away. Basic breathing skills can be learned and used within minutes. Or there are more complex techniques which you can become skilled at gradually over weeks, months, or even years, like t'ai chi or meditation. Then you can choose between the traditional and the alternative, or there's even the high tech if that's your preference. Many people find themselves using a mixture of all of these. You can 'do-it for yourself' using music, meditation, breathing, or a wide range of straightforward practical methods, or enlist the assistance of a therapist and have an aromatherapy massage, acupuncture or reiki session. The beauty of it is that you can try any or all of these to see what works for you. And it's best not to prejudge anything in the art of relaxation. You can never tell what might do it for you. You might just surprise yourself.

You can also choose to work on your whole body and mind, or focus on just one area: your body, your mind, shoulders, face, back, neck muscles, head, whatever. Perhaps you just want to know how to deal with panic attacks, anger or anxiety. Many people would like to learn how to relax better in particular situations like exams, meetings, or coping with a difficult line manager or other colleague. For others, all they need is help getting off to a good night's sleep.

So, there truly is something for everyone in learning how to relax. You are spoilt for choice. But there may be just one more thing you're going to have to do to make a proper start. You may still have to allow yourself the time and the space in your life to learn, and to use this new skill. You may need to make your quality of life a priority, and find time just for you, and only you. That's not selfish. Because doing this will make you a stronger, healthier, happier and more reliable person. And this will not only have countless benefits for you, but also for those you come into contact with, every single day.

Take a few minutes now and try these simple techniques.

For your face and forehead

Take the second and third fingers of each hand and rest them gently on your temples. Now, with eyes closed, lightly massage this area with slow, small circular movements.

For your whole body

Make a tight fist with both hands, curl your toes up really tight, hunch up your shoulders, press your lips together hard ... and hold all of that tightly for about ten seconds. Then ... release all of that tension completely, and let it all go. Allow the resulting feeling of relaxation to spread through your whole body.

There is so much you can do to bring calmness and well-being to your entire body and mind. It's just about knowing how.

1

Relaxation – a skill with a long history

In this chapter you will learn:
- *about the benefits of relaxation*
- *the many uses of relaxation*
- *easy and quick ways to relax*
- *about the early beginnings of relaxation.*

As long as you live, keep learning how to live.

Seneca, Roman dramatist, poet and statesman (circa 4 BC–65 AD)

Learning is an intrinsic and natural part of life. It is as old as life itself. From the instant of our birth, we are active learners, hungry for knowledge, and motivated to understand what goes on around us. We automatically strive to make sense of the jumble of information reaching our brand new and very acute senses. We learn so much without even noticing we are doing it. Learning new things is part of what makes us human; humanity has always had a drive to learn.

The *Teach Yourself* series of books provides a forum for learning a wide variety of new skills, or acquiring new knowledge and understanding of a huge array of topics. In this book, you will be able to teach yourself how to relax, and be able to pass on this information to family and friends, should you want to. Learning to relax is not something new. Although it may seem to be something we associate with today's rapid pace of life, and the stresses and strains of twenty-first century living, the art of relaxation has a very long history, and these skills can be found stretching back many centuries, and to many diverse parts of the world. The journey through life has clearly never been an easy one.

For example, the organized practice of meditation is thought to go back at least 5,000 years to its development in India. It is even thought that meditation may have developed as long ago as when early humans stared into the flames of their fires for long periods of time, and fell into a state of relaxation. Acupuncture originated in China, some 5,000 years ago. The practice of t'ai chi (pronounced 'ty chee') originated in China and has been in use there for many centuries. It involves slow, rhythmic movements of the body, which are believed to help calm the mind and relax the muscles and nervous system.

Benefits of relaxation

Relaxation is a tremendously effective antidote to tension and stress, and it has the added advantages of being straightforward to learn and having no side effects. But it is not just about relieving tension and stress. Being relaxed and at ease has many, many benefits in its own right, even if you are not stressed or tense to begin with. Being able to achieve a state of complete relaxation in mind and body has numerous benefits for us all, whether thousands of years ago, or today. This means that no matter what your reason for wanting to learn this exciting and most rewarding of arts, there is so much that you can get out of it.

Research, evidence and statistics

A four-year research study funded by the NHS in the 1990s showed that patients who were attending their GP because they were stressed had found that regular relaxation had the most effect in reducing their tension and stress.

The most profound benefits relaxation can bring are those relating to you as a person, the whole you, the inner you – your core being if you like. Here are just some of the benefits which relaxing regularly can bring to you:

▸ *calmness*
▸ *stillness*
▸ *inner glow*
▸ *inner strength*
▸ *togetherness*
▸ *contentment*
▸ *completeness*
▸ *confidence*
▸ *positivity*
▸ *peace*
▸ *fulfilment*
▸ *feeling in control of yourself and your life*
▸ *cushioning from stress*
▸ *it just feels really good.*

Apart from these holistic effects, being able to relax can also help you to deal much more effectively and successfully with all sorts of situations that may arise in everyday life. Here are some examples:

▸ *exams or tests*
▸ *interviews*
▸ *making a presentation*
▸ *making a complaint*
▸ *if you are angry or frustrated*
▸ *if someone else is angry with* **you**
▸ *your driving test*
▸ *at the dentist*
▸ *when you can't sleep*
▸ *an argument or difference of opinion*
▸ *being criticized, fairly or unfairly*
▸ *taking something back to a shop*
▸ *if you feel panicky or nervous*

- *at work in general*
- *appraisals at work*
- *being a parent*
- *being a carer.*

Relaxation can have beneficial effects on immune and psychological well-being.

Dr Janice Kiecolt-Glaser, Professor of Psychology and Psychiatry,

Ohio State University (1999)

YOUR RELATIONSHIPS

In your relationships, an ability to stay calm and unruffled means that you can deal more effectively with whatever life throws up for you. This might be with family, friends, your partner, neighbours, or at work. An added bonus is that if we are calm, this rubs off on those around us too, making them feel calmer, more in control and more confident – colleagues, employees, partner, children, friends, and so on. In this way you are teaching by example, something which shouldn't be underestimated. You can even take things a stage further, and if someone in your circle of family and friends is struggling to cope with tension or stress, or one of the situations already mentioned, you can teach them what you learn from this book.

Insight

Life, family and friends are special and wonderful gifts. It seems to me that learning how to relax will help you to make so much more of these, and even to be able to help a friend in need.

Try this – Letting go

1 *In your own time, breathe in slowly, and as you do so, silently scan and check over your body for any tension. Shoulders, hands, back, neck, jaw, head, legs, feet... wherever. Notice where there is any tension.*

YOUR HEALTH

Being able to unwind and relax, on a daily basis, also brings
with it profound and wide-reaching health benefits. If you have
frequent colds, sore throats or other illnesses, your immune
system may not be as strong as it might be. Relaxation has been
shown to strengthen your immune response. It can also enhance
your general sense of well-being. There is evidence confirming
benefits in the following areas of health for most people who
maintain a regular relaxation programme or, better still, build it
in to their everyday life:

▶ *Healthy blood pressure is maintained.*
▶ *Cardiovascular health (heart, circulation etc.) is improved.*
▶ *The immune system is strengthened.*
▶ *Energy levels are improved.*
▶ *A feeling of overall health and well-being is achieved.*

**Relaxation techniques are often taught in antenatal
classes. Being able to relax during labour helps conserve
energy, reduce pain and maximize the oxygen supply
to the baby.**

National Childbirth Trust

Uses of relaxation

There are so many uses for relaxation, with more being added
all the time. Most smoking cessation programmes now include
teaching relaxation as a way of coping better with the cravings
and general agitation brought about by trying to stop smoking.
Audiologists find relaxation can be helpful for the many people

who are troubled by constant sounds in their ears (tinnitus). Studies also show that those with depression, or chronic fatigue syndrome (also known as ME or Myalgic Encephalomyelitis), can have their symptoms improved if they use relaxation regularly. Here are just some of the applications relaxation has been used for. These will be discussed in more detail in later chapters:

▶ *stress*
▶ *depression*
▶ *postnatal depression*
▶ *insomnia*
▶ *tension*
▶ *migraine*
▶ *childbirth*
▶ *anxiety*
▶ *pain management*
▶ *ME (Myalgic Encephalomyelitis)*
▶ *anger management*
▶ *stopping smoking*
▶ *tinnitus*
▶ *IBS (irritable bowel syndrome)*
▶ *panic attacks*
▶ *phobias and OCD (obsessive-compulsive disorder).*

A good relaxation technique is a weapon that you always carry with you, to help you deal with any situation as it arises. Make relaxation a regular part of your daily routine. There are so many relaxation techniques, from deep breathing and visualization to meditation and self-hypnosis. Find one that works for you.

International Stress Management Association (ISMA) UK, 2008

How to relax

Most people can relax with a good book or TV programme, or by having a long lazy bath, maybe pottering in the garden or tinkering with the car in the garage, going for a run or a walk on the beach, or walking the dog. And this works for many people, depending on their personal interests and preferences. Recent research has even shown that stroking a friendly cat or dog, preferably your own, has a noticeably calming effect, and can even lower blood pressure.

But sometimes these everyday activities just don't work. If tension is acute and happens frequently, you can't always be reading a book, going for a walk, or listening to music. There is life to get on with, and work to be done. Such activities are usually very time-consuming, and there aren't enough hours in the day. And if you're at work or out shopping, or driving, or looking after children or an elderly person, what do you do then?

That's why this book is so important. You will learn how to relax anywhere, anytime, in quick ways, and in slow ways, using skills you can put into action while you're doing something else and, of course, there will be a wide variety of long, slow techniques for you to choose from, for when you have that extra time and space. Relaxation is often referred to as 'exercises', but this is not really the case. 'Techniques' or 'methods' is much nearer to the reality of it. Most involve very little physical input. None are at all strenuous. Some are only using your breathing or thinking. So there should be something for everyone, and you don't have to be particularly fit for any of them. If you are at all concerned about any technique, just check with your doctor before you go ahead. Relaxation is not a difficult skill to learn – it's just about knowing how.

A FEW WORDS OF CAUTION

Firstly, as just described, this book will cover a wide range of relaxation techniques, with varied physical input. The most you are likely to be asked to do is tense a set of muscles, say, make a tight fist with your hand. But if you are in any doubt at all about your fitness to use or try out a technique or method, then it is best not to go ahead with it. There will be lots of other alternatives offered, so you won't be missing out. Or you can adapt the activity to suit your particular needs. If it still works for you with your adaptation, then it is still going to be beneficial to you. It's as simple as that.

Stephen Palmer of the London Centre for Stress Management agrees that care should be exercised by some people. There can be an initial increase in blood pressure brought about by tensing the muscles, so if this could be a problem, it makes sense to avoid methods which involve this. In addition, there is a very small minority, usually those with an anxiety problem, who may feel panicky when first using techniques involving relaxation or breathing exercises. Regular practice should sort out this last difficulty fairly quickly. You can always check with your doctor or other health professional if you're not sure about a particular technique.

Secondly, relaxation can bring huge benefits but it is not a miracle cure. If you are finding any of the following are causing you a problem or placing limitations on your life, then contact your GP, who will be able to offer you support and advice:

▶ *panic attacks*
▶ *depressed or low mood*
▶ *stress*
▶ *anxiety*
▶ *tension*
▶ *phobia*
▶ *obsessional or compulsive behaviour*
▶ *obsessional or compulsive thinking.*

But, for the vast majority of people, relaxation should not present any problems and provide nothing but benefits, with absolutely no side effects. This book will give you numerous types and techniques to try out, so that you can enjoy finding out which suit you best.

Try this – Slow down

1 *Sit comfortably and quietly, and bring your thoughts to yourself, just sitting there.*
2 *Close your eyes gently, and become aware of your breathing. Take a gentle breath in, and in your own time, sigh it back out, allowing your shoulders to relax.*
3 *Now in your own time, as you breathe in, silently place the word 'SLOW' on your inward breath, and as you breathe out, place the word 'DOWN' on your outward breath.*
4 *Repeat this for one or two minutes.*

Insight

This is a very busy world, and it's easy to lose sight of where you're actually going. When you relax, it's as if the world is standing still to give you a chance to think.

Why telling yourself to relax is difficult

As newborn infants, we are completely able to relax. It comes absolutely automatically to us, as we lie secure and at ease in our mother's arms. Provided we are fed, warm, dry and emotionally secure, relaxing is what a new baby does best, and does for most of the time. Toddlers playing on a swing or a chute, or in the paddling pool, can still just relax and enjoy themselves without thinking about it. And yet, somewhere along the line, by the time we are adults, or even before that, many people find that trying to relax can be very difficult, if not impossible. You know what you want to do. You sit down and try to relax. But your mind and body just don't seem to want to comply. There are two reasons for this:

▶ *One is that we can actually forget how to relax.*
▶ *And second, you can't just tell your body to relax.*

Over months or years of feeling tense or stressed, day in and day out, we become accustomed to feeling tense. We begin to believe that it is normal to feel that way. We can actually forget how to relax. One way of thinking about it is that the pathways in our brain which lead to relaxation have become overgrown and impassable, whereas the pathways leading to tension are clear and well-maintained motorways.

The second reason is due to the way our body works. The part of our body which makes us relax is the same part which makes us breathe, and makes our heart beat. It's sometimes likened to an 'automatic pilot'. We can't tell our heart to beat, or to beat faster when we have to climb some stairs. It just happens 'automatically'. So, in the same way, we can't tell our body or our mind to relax. They won't hear us. They are set in 'tense' mode. It would be like telling the automatic pilot on a plane to change direction. It just can't be done. But there are many ways to speak our body's language, and to communicate with both mind and body, asking them to relax. And that's what this book will teach you. Manual override if you like.

For many people the straightforward answer is to spend time regularly on a practical activity which reduces arousal and tension in the muscles. Most people would find it relatively easy to find a suitable activity: a warm lazy bath, listening to a favourite piece of music, aromatherapy, a walk on the beach, yoga, gardening, dancing, sport, and so on. The choice of activity is very much down to personal taste and effectiveness.

However, there can be several drawbacks with this approach:

- ▶ *If you are very tense, arousal and tension may be so persistent that the muscles need to be relaxed frequently, several times a day or more.*
- ▶ *If you are very tense, this kind of approach may not work.*
- ▶ *Arousal and tension often occur while you are doing something else, such as in the workplace, or out socially.*
- ▶ *You may not be able to find an everyday activity which relaxes you.*
- ▶ *Most of these activities are very time-consuming.*

Research, evidence and statistics

In 1996, a team from Boston College School of Nursing,
Massachusetts, USA (Mandle, Jacobs, Arcari and Domar),
reported the findings of their review of 37 separate studies
looking at the effectiveness of relaxation for adults. The
results consistently suggest the effectiveness of relaxation
in reducing hypertension, insomnia, anxiety, pain and
medication use.

Relaxation techniques

Simple and non-strenuous relaxation techniques are a convenient
alternative. This idea dates back to 1938 in Chicago, when
Dr Edmund Jacobson introduced 'progressive relaxation', which
is effective even for severe tension. He and his colleagues had
noticed that their patients' knee-jerk reaction was stronger the
more tense the patient was. Jacobson went on to develop a method
which demonstrated that if a muscle is first tensed, it will then
automatically relax. Regular practice was required to acquire this
skill. His patients would progressively tense then relax each muscle
group in turn, until their whole body was relaxed and arousal
reduced.

Since then, methods of relaxing without first tensing the muscles
have been developed, including techniques to relax the mind as
well as the body. With practice, these techniques can be used

quickly and effectively in almost any situation. If you are at work, you can use the shorter techniques at lunchtime, or during coffee breaks, or even while doing your job, with longer sessions saved for later on at home.

'Biofeedback' devices have also been introduced which involve giving some sort of 'feedback' on your tension and arousal level in the form of sound or a light display. This lets you know immediately that what you are doing is relaxing you, so this encourages you to continue and the process of relaxation will continue. Many people particularly enjoy this method, and enjoy watching the pointer fall or the sound level reduce on the particular equipment they are using. These devices are available from specialist suppliers at varying cost, some relatively inexpensive. Various computerized versions are also now available, though these tend to be more expensive. More about this in a later chapter.

With practice, many of these techniques can achieve relaxation in as little as a few minutes, or seconds. This book will allow you to try out a range of these relaxation techniques, to find the one which is most practical, enjoyable and effective for you. Whichever you choose, it should be used regularly, at first to acquire the skill, then to cushion the effects of tension by reducing and discouraging arousal.

HOW OFTEN SHOULD YOU RELAX?

There are no set rules or guidelines on this. It all depends on what your starting point is, why you are doing it, what method you are using and what you want to get out of it. There are many techniques described in this book, and each will give some idea of how often and when to use it. But to give an idea, here are some examples:

1 *Jack enjoys life, and goes to a t'ai chi class for two hours every week, because he enjoys it and finds it peaceful.*
2 *Debra finds her work a bit stressful sometimes, so she has a long relaxation session one evening a week, followed by a lazy bath.*

3 Denise has young children and feels tense all the time, so she has bought a relaxation DVD and follows the programme for ten minutes every evening when the children are in bed.

4 Joe just enjoys chilling out as it makes him feel good, and gives him more energy, so he uses a relaxation technique for about 15 minutes before dinner most nights.

5 Pauline is very stressed at work, and uses quick ways of relaxing using her breathing, several times a day. She also goes to a yoga class every Tuesday evening.

6 Lee has no particular problems with tension or stress, but just wants to be as relaxed as he can be, so he uses computer programmes specially designed for this, two or three times a week.

Insight

As evening approaches, make it a habit to think about the positive things which have happened to you that day. They needn't be big, little things will do. I find this brings me renewed strength, added energy and a warm feeling inside.

ONE CHANGE AT A TIME

You should find lots which will appeal to you in this book. And by all means give everything a try, to see how effective it is. Everyone is different. It's not one size fits all when it comes to relaxation. But it is advisable not to make too many changes all at once. Only make one change at a time if you want it to last. Only build one new skill in to your life at a time. There's not only you who will be aware of changes, there are those around you too. Trying to change too much all at once is itself going to add to tension and stress so, like learning anything new, it's best to take one careful step at a time, make sure you have learned and established that, and then move on to the next. You will get there more quickly and more surely in the end.

KEY POINTS

Look back over this chapter and choose the FOUR pieces of information you found to be most interesting or helpful. Write these here, or go back and underline or highlight them in some way.

1 ....

2 ....

3 ....

4 ....

Look back over this chapter and choose the FOUR practical suggestions you found to be most useful. Write these here, or go back and underline or highlight them in some way.

1 ....

2 ....

3 ....

4 ....

Which TWO techniques or suggestions from this chapter would you like to try out straight away?

Write these here, or go back and underline or highlight them in some way.

1 ....

2 ....

Which FOUR techniques or suggestions from this chapter would you like to work towards using regularly?

Write these here, or go back and underline or highlight them in some way.

1 ....

2 ....

3 ....

4 ....

2

Relaxation, stress and tension explained

In this chapter you will learn:
- *about tension, relaxation and stress – what they are and how they are linked*
- *what panic is and how to deal with it*
- *easy and quick ways to relax*
- *what happens to your 'brainwaves' when you relax.*

What is relaxation?

Complete relaxation could be thought of as a state of deep and complete rest and calm, when your entire mind and body are completely in balance, and completely at ease. The more you relax, the more your muscles release tension, and your organs slow down. Blood flow to the brain increases. As the muscles relax, the brain even releases the body's own natural opiates, called endorphins. These are pain-relieving hormones that are related to synthetic opiates like morphine. Endorphins can be released by any number of stimuli, including laughter and exercise. That release is at the heart of relaxation techniques and the relaxation response, and is why relaxation feels good.

When the relaxation response is activated:

- ▶ *the body prepares for rest*
- ▶ *blood pressure decreases or stabilizes*
- ▶ *muscle tension decreases*
- ▶ *pupils get smaller*
- ▶ *air passages narrow*
- ▶ *blood flow to muscles decreases*
- ▶ *blood flow to extremities increases*
- ▶ *bladder muscles and tubes relax*
- ▶ *perspiration decreases*
- ▶ *pulse rate decreases*
- ▶ *saliva flow increases*
- ▶ *stomach and digestion activity increases*
- ▶ *brain relaxes*
- ▶ *metabolic rate decreases*
- ▶ *breathing rate decreases*
- ▶ *breathing becomes less shallow*
- ▶ *blood glucose and fats normalize*
- ▶ *lactic acid levels decrease*
- ▶ *anxiety levels decrease.*

Your body begins to move from a state of physiological arousal, ready for whatever action is required, to a state of physiological relaxation, where blood pressure, breathing and heart rate, and digestive functioning return to their relaxed state. Releasing muscle tension is in itself a relief from pain and discomfort. You could liken this to a row of soldiers, primed and ready for action, being told 'At ease'.

Insight

Wherever you are today, at work, in town, or at home, try noticing all the little things. Look around yourself, and take in those interesting, curious, funny, bright, colourful or lovely things, which usually just pass you by. If you can do that, even for a few moments, you'll feel more alive and more in harmony with your world.

In addition to its calming physical effects, research has shown that the relaxation response also increases energy and focus, combats illness, relieves aches and pains, heightens problem-solving abilities, and boosts motivation and productivity.

The stress response

The body uses countless chemical messengers in the blood to produce effects in organs all round the body. These chemical messengers are called hormones. You will probably be familiar with hormones such as oestrogen and testosterone, the sex hormones. But there are numerous other hormones, all with a specific job to do in the body. Adrenalin and cortisol are also hormones, with their own specific effects.

During stress, the adrenal glands release adrenalin into the bloodstream, along with other hormones like cortisol, signalling the heart to pump harder, increasing blood pressure, opening airways in the lungs, increasing blood flow to major muscle groups, and performing other functions to enable the body to fight or run when encountering a perceived threat. This ancient mechanism developed in prehistoric times to deal with a physical threat such as a sabre-toothed tiger or a venomous snake, but can just as easily be triggered today by situations in which we feel threatened as a person. Examples of this might be when criticized at work, having an argument with a partner, or being faced with a mountain of bills to pay. You could think of this as a psychological threat, rather than a physical one.

Cortisol is a hormone produced by the adrenal glands. It helps regulate blood pressure and heart function, as well as the body's use of proteins, carbohydrates and fats. The secretion of cortisol increases in response to physical and psychological stress during the **fight or flight response**, which is why it is sometimes called 'the stress hormone'.

In the brain, the major players in the acute stress response are the hypothalamus and the pituitary gland, both deep in the brain, but close to one another. The **hypothalamus** is a hollow, funnel-shaped part of the brain, with the **pituitary gland**, a pea-shaped structure, located just below it. In addition to many other roles, the hypothalamus regulates certain activities of the autonomic nervous system (ANS), via the pituitary. The pituitary secretes a range of these 'chemical messengers' called hormones, which are sent through the bloodstream to encourage other target organs to come into action – a kind of command and control function, using hormones as a sort of remote control to make changes.

In the case of perceived threat or tension, the hypothalamus triggers the pituitary to secrete a specific hormone called adrenocorticotropic hormone, or ACTH, into the bloodstream, which in turn stimulates the adrenal glands to produce adrenalin and cortisol. The adrenal glands are small pyramidal organs located at the top of each kidney. It's all a kind of domino effect, with perceived stress starting it off. This system is part of a more wide-ranging system which controls and regulates various body processes including digestion, the immune system, mood, sexuality and energy usage. It's not specific to threat or danger.

Brainwaves

The brain is an extremely complex and very clever organ, its many functions going on seamlessly, all at one time, maintaining balance and keeping our bodies and minds working efficiently. Another way of looking at relaxation is to move sideways from the chemical level of hormones, which we've just been examining, to look at what is happening at the brainwave level.

You may be surprised to find that there is electrical activity going on in our brains all the time. This is very low voltage activity of course, nothing like the strength of the electrical supply we use every day, but easily measurable. The reason this activity is called waves, is because it is a bit like waves on the sea, some being shallower and faster, and some being deep and slow.

Wave name	Number every second (approx)	Associated with
Delta	1–4	Deep sleep.
Theta	5–7	Just falling asleep.
Alpha	8–14	Relaxed but alert. Not working on any task in particular. Pleasant and relaxed feelings.
Beta	15–35	Very alert. Concentrating on a demanding task. Common during anxiety or panic attacks.

So what you are aiming for in relaxing is to encourage the brain to move from producing mainly Beta waves, to producing mainly Alpha waves. You want to be relaxed, but still awake. This is similar to meditation, and is more easily achieved with your eyes closed. If your eyes are open, watching a scene such as waves lapping quietly on the seashore, or a beautiful and large-scale landscape such as rolling hills, lakes or mountains can be helpful. You can also use a picture, a video/DVD, or a computer program to simulate these for you. There is a wide range of merchandise currently available to help with this. More on this in Chapter 10, and in the 'Taking it further' section at the end of the book.

If getting to sleep is a problem, what you really need to do is start off by using relaxation to help you to achieve Alpha waves. So you want to wind down slowly from the Beta waves which are keeping you awake, slowly into Alpha, and then if you continue relaxing even more deeply, into Theta, and then into the welcome Delta waves of deep and refreshing sleep. Trying to move straight from Beta to Delta is too much to ask any brain to manage.

Getting tension levels right

But being relaxed is not just about the complete absence of tension. Whatever we do requires a certain amount of tension in our muscles. Imagine trying to stand without there being tension in the muscles of our legs, back and feet, to hold us upright. Holding the telephone or a coffee cup requires just the right pattern of tension in the appropriate muscles. Too little and we would drop what we were holding, too much and we might crush the delicate flower we had just picked from the garden. Everything we do uses a set of muscles, and tension is a necessary part of that – walking, speaking, eating, indeed everything we do. It's alright to be completely relaxed if you are lying down in bed or on the beach, but for most of our lives it's about getting the level of tension just right. Not too much, and not too little.

Having too little tension is rarely a problem in our everyday lives. Muscle weakness is more likely to be brought on by an illness of some kind, which lowers our energy levels, or has affected our muscles or the messages reaching them from the brain, like in MS or motor neurone disease.

What we are looking for is a careful balance. It's all about having the right amount of muscle tension for the job in hand. Yerkes and Dodson explained this with their well-known 'arousal curve' in 1908. 'Arousal' of the body refers to the state of readiness to respond to a task. They explained that if physiological arousal was too high or too low, then performance on a task would be poor, as shown in Figure 2.1.

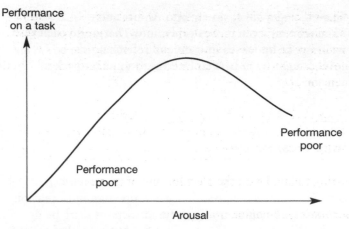

Figure 2.1 *How physiological arousal affects performance.*

You could think of physiological arousal, effort and tension as being very similar. We require little effort to watch TV or read a book, so the optimum levels of arousal and tension are low. But if we have to dig the garden or play squash, we need much more effort, we need to be much more ready for action, and we also need much more muscle tension. But in any of these cases, we can have more than enough tension, and so be overworking our body unnecessarily. It is this *extra* tension which is a problem, and is so typical of when we are stressed or under pressure, or scared or worried. And this extra tension can produce painful muscles at the end of the day, and make us feel much more tired than we need to be.

Try this – Detecting your levels

How do you know if you have too much tension? Begin to notice your muscles. We are usually too busy and preoccupied with other things to notice what our muscles are doing. Think about it now...

Focus on the muscles in your fingers... your arms... your shoulders... your back... the back of your neck... Are they relaxed? Are they just right? Or do they feel too tense for what you're doing? If so, let the extra tension go.

Then there's your face... and your forehead. There can be so much tension here. Scan them now... round your eyes... round your mouth... your cheeks... your nose... your forehead. More tense than they need to be? Let that tension go.

Start noticing these things today. Release any unnecessary tension you notice. Become much more self-aware. And you will become more relaxed.

Starting today, be on the alert for any of these:

- *holding the phone too tightly*
- *clenching your teeth*
- *arching your back while driving*
- *grinding your teeth at night*
- *holding your coffee cup, glass, or the steering wheel too tightly*
- *nail marks in the palm of your hand from clenching your fist (day or night)*
- *tongue pressed against the roof of your mouth*
- *gripping your pen or the mouse too tightly*
- *hitting the keyboard keys harder than you need to*
- *holding your child's hand too tightly*
- *being too tense when you walk*
- *having your arms folded tightly*
- *gripping the supermarket trolley more than necessary*
- *crossing your legs too tightly, or winding them round each other.*

Having more tension than you need can produce unexplained aches and pains, or tingling and numbness, especially in the neck, shoulders and back, usually in the evening when you relax, or the next day. Feeling off balance when standing or walking can be caused by having more tension in one shoulder than in the other, or across your back, giving you an imbalance when you sit, stand or walk. This can feel very odd and unsettling.

Causes of tension

PACE OF LIFE

The pace of life is so fast today, and so much is packed into each day, that it's easy to find yourself going anything from a little too fast, to flat out. What with traffic jams, packed or delayed trains and buses, queues at the bank or the supermarket, to name but a few examples, it can be difficult to even know what a 'normal' pace might be like. It's common to have forgotten what a normal pace of life or work actually feels like, and to have become accustomed to this faster pace. But this brings extra tension with it. Can you identify with any of these?

- *eating too fast – do you finish a meal before everyone else?*
- *hurrying round the shops*
- *shovelling food in without tasting it*
- *talking too quickly*
- *chewing too fast*
- *hoovering, ironing or dusting at breakneck speed*
- *dressing in a rush*
- *dressing the children in a rush*
- *driving too fast*
- *eating on the run – never sitting down to eat at a table*
- *swallowing food before it's properly chewed*
- *rushing out of the front door to go to work*
- *making your children do things quickly*
- *rushing home to get the meal on*

> ▸ *rushing to collect the kids or drop them off somewhere*
> ▸ *hurrying out to meet friends.*

EMOTIONS

Sometimes it's just the way you are feeling that can produce too much muscle tension. It's not so much what you are doing, or who you are with, it's about what's going on inside your head, and in your heart. It's about feelings and emotions. Any of the following will make you more tense than necessary:

▸ *stress*
▸ *anger*
▸ *resentment*
▸ *jealousy*
▸ *frustration*
▸ *impatience*
▸ *hurt*
▸ *boredom*
▸ *fear*
▸ *disappointment*
▸ *anxiety or worry*
▸ *bereavement.*

STRESS

When we are stressed, as we have seen, the automatic part of our nervous system becomes aroused. That's the part which keeps us breathing and our heart beating automatically, without us having to think about it. This arousal is a necessary part of our biological make-up, and evolved in our caveman ancestors as a self-preservation mechanism, to prepare them to cope *physically* with whatever dangerous situation they might experience.

So, in the case of an approaching snarling sabre-toothed tiger, this instant automatic arousal prepared our ancestors to either 'fight' the animal, or 'flee' as fast as they could. This all happened completely automatically, because if our ancestors had taken time to think about it, it would have been too late. Every split second counted in our early days. So we breathe faster, think faster, our heart beats faster, our muscles become taut and ready for action, our blood sugar levels rise to give rapid energy, increased amounts of adrenalin are produced, and so on. All to prepare us for instant and effective action. And this is the source of tension.

In terms of evolution, this development was all relatively recent, so our bodies react in exactly the same way today. However, in our modern world, stress does not usually arise from *physically* dangerous situations. We can't fight with our line manager, or run away from our debts, much as we might want to. In today's world there is seldom a *physical* outlet for the ancient 'fight or flight' reaction and the arousal it produces. So, all those major bodily changes have no outlet, leaving you feeling very strange indeed. If the reaction is particularly strong, you can experience this as a panic attack, or anxiety attack. Also, stress today can be a long-term problem, going on for weeks or months without a break. Your nervous system can then become stuck in a groove, with tension continuing long after the situation provoking it has disappeared, leaving you stuck with the outcome of a stressful situation which has passed long ago.

What we are describing here is a normal physical reaction, something we share with all other animals. Everyone has this response to danger, so there is in fact nothing physically wrong if you are stressed. You don't have a disease. Stress isn't an illness. Stress can make you feel really ill though, even though you aren't, strictly speaking, ill. The stress reaction can ruin and limit your life, and change the way you present yourself to the world. You need to turn it down, like turning down the volume control of an annoying radio.

> *Before you agree to do anything that might add even the smallest amount of stress to your life ... give yourself time to let a yes resound within you. When it's right, I guarantee that your entire body will feel it.*
>
> Oprah Winfrey, US talk-show host (1954–)

What is stress?

It's difficult these days not to see a newspaper article, or come across a radio or TV programme discussing stress. It would appear to be on the increase, and most of us will know someone who is stressed. Most people, when they are stressed, also tend to be anxious. So stress and anxiety usually go hand in hand. You may feel that you are not stressed, but if you are at all anxious, there will be something in your life which is a stressor for you. You may just not be aware of what it is.

There are many, many ways of defining what stress is. We've looked at this at the brain chemistry level, and also in relation to brainwave activity. Here is another more familiar way of looking at it. At its simplest, stress is when people feel pressure because of circumstances which make them feel one or more of these:

- ▶ *threatened*
- ▶ *unsure or unfamiliar*
- ▶ *overwhelmed*
- ▶ *trapped*
- ▶ *dissatisfied or unhappy*
- ▶ *that they can't cope as well as they want to*
- ▶ *that they can't cope at all.*

Though this is a definition of stress, it reads just like a description of what it feels like to lack confidence. So it's not surprising that low confidence often goes hand in hand with stress.

SIGNS OF STRESS

As described earlier, stress upsets the normal body chemistry throughout the whole body. This inevitably produces all sorts of symptoms. Here are some of the signs and symptoms of stress. They are divided into three types for simplicity.

Physical

- ▶ *headaches*
- ▶ *indigestion/churning stomach*
- ▶ *palpitations*
- ▶ *difficulty taking a deep breath*
- ▶ *difficulty swallowing*
- ▶ *nausea*
- ▶ *tiredness*
- ▶ *aches and pains*
- ▶ *muscle twitches*
- ▶ *sweating*
- ▶ *muscle tension*
- ▶ *weight gain or loss*
- ▶ *trembling*
- ▶ *dry mouth*
- ▶ *tingling in fingers, toes and face.*

Emotional

- ▶ *irritability*
- ▶ *forgetfulness*
- ▶ *panicky*
- ▶ *gloomy thoughts*
- ▶ *fearfulness*
- ▶ *anxiety/worry*
- ▶ *depression*
- ▶ *negative thinking*
- ▶ *feeling 'unreal'.*

Behaviour

- ▶ *nail-biting*
- ▶ *restlessness*
- ▶ *agitation*
- ▶ *can't sleep or very sleepy*
- ▶ *eating too much or too little*
- ▶ *making mistakes*
- ▶ *poor concentration*
- ▶ *change in usual behaviour*
- ▶ *indecision*
- ▶ *anger*

- *forgetfulness*
- *increases in smoking or drinking.*

STRESS IS NORMAL

Saying that stress is normal is not to underestimate the immensity of the problems it produces and the misery it can cause. Stress can affect your life adversely through no fault of your own. No one should feel guilty about being stressed, because the most able, most sensitive, and even the rich and famous can all suffer from stress. A day seldom goes by these days without the newspapers reporting another celebrity checking into a clinic for this reason.

Stress is normal, except that sometimes it may go over the top and occur too severely, in the wrong places, at the wrong times and it can take over your life. It's then that it is best to seek professional help from your doctor.

STRESS FROM 'GOOD EVENTS'

Having said all this, stress is not always connected to bad things. Even what has been planned as a 'happy' event such as a wedding, the birth of a baby, or a new house or business can be just as stressful. This is because of the extra workload, costs, deadlines to meet, unclear outcomes and life changes they bring about.

Also, we all need a certain amount of challenge and stimulation in our lives, but if this gets too much for us, we can then feel stressed too. These ideas have given rise to a common perception that some stress is good for you. This could not be more wrong. Stress is about overload and inability to cope. This is never good. Yes, we need challenge, stimulation and excitement in our lives. But we don't need stress.

Insight
Keep your eye on what's important. Don't get too bogged down in the everyday grind, which can so dominate our lives today. I like to keep an eye on those twinkling stars too.

Are we more stressed today?

Every period of human history has produced its own problems, be it famine, war, disease, pestilence or flood. So should there not be less stress nowadays instead of more, with relatively few of such dreadful and life-threatening problems to face here in the West? The simple answer is no, we are actually more at the mercy of stress today for several reasons.

First of all, in historical times, society was less complex, and the episodes of stress were in the main few and far between, and coming in short powerful bursts. War, pestilence or indeed any of these major stressors might never reach your small corner of the world. This compares with the much more damaging, ever-present, long-term stress of today's sophisticated, high-speed, global existence.

Then there's the fact that even during the two World Wars of the twentieth century, people used to have a sense of being part of one nation with everyone on the same side, pulling together and supporting one another. In the Depression of the 1930s, millions of people felt that they were fighting the same fight, shoulder to shoulder. This feeling of being in it together, and not being isolated, has the effect of considerably reducing the adverse effects of a time of great stress. Being alone with a stress can make it so very much more intense and unremitting.

Added to this there's the pressure of time. Today we are very much ruled by the clock, with unrelenting time pressure placed upon many of us. In previous centuries, and even as late as the 1950s, all that mattered was that it was early morning, or lunchtime, or mid-afternoon. Now we need to know that it is exactly 3.25 p.m., and that we still have two meetings to fit in, or there's still the shopping to be done and the children to be picked up from school.

And of course there's the way that life today is ever-changing, and even the rate of change is on the increase. But change is by its very nature stressful. We constantly have to make readjustments to our lives, and all of these changes produce another small injection of arousal and stress.

Finally, think about this. Every historical period, and every society has its own idea of what life and human nature is all about. Current Western society emphasizes the importance of the successful and independent individual, exercising choice and making decisions in a world where possessions matter. This automatically places continuous stress on people to strive for material success – the rat race, in other words. But this emphasis on the successful individual is by no means a universal concept. Other societies past and present do not share this view of life. In some cultures, it's the community or society itself which is considered to be more important, or the good we do for others, or in some cases the individual and their society can be blurred into one. The Javanese, for example, believe that all expression of individual importance is impolite and vulgar. While not suggesting that everyone moves to Java to escape stress, we must recognize that stress is very much an outcome of the nature of twenty-first century life in a Western-style society.

Research, evidence and statistics

▶ *The 2006/2007 survey of 'Self-reported Work-related Illness' indicated that around 530,000 individuals in Britain believed that they were experiencing work-related stress at a level that was making them ill.*

(Contd)

Stress and anxiety

It's very difficult to explain the difference between stress and anxiety.
The two are sometimes used interchangeably. Everything that has been
said about stress, will also apply to anxiety. If someone is stressed,
one of the key signs of this stress is likely to be anxiety. Anxiety is
often called worry, but unlike worry, it may not always be directed
at anything in particular. You can worry about your job, or how you
are going to pay all those bills, but sometimes you can feel anxious,
or worried, and not be able to put your finger on why. This can be
particularly upsetting, as it can all seem so puzzling and unexplained.

Try this – How stressed are you?

Think about your own life just now. On a piece of paper,
or in a notebook, write down everything you can think of
which could be causing you unhelpful stress or tension at the
moment (think about people, work, family, relationships,
events, daily hassles, problems etc.), as shown below. Now
rate each on a scale of 1–10 (10 being the maximum stress you
can imagine) of how stressful it is:

Item	Stress rating from 1–10
Total stress rating	

Take your time, and allow yourself to become aware of all stressors in your life. Add others in now if you've missed any out. Now total these up to give an idea of the potential for unhelpful stress in your life. Bear in mind that the ideal score here would be zero, as we are clearly thinking about unhelpful stress. We prefer to think that all stress is unhelpful, and that the popular idea of there being 'useful stress', to spur us on to greater things, is better thought of as 'challenge' or 'stimulation', which we all need in life.

Insight

It's so very easy to focus on the stresses and strains and forget the positives and good in our lives, no matter how small. But if we ignore the positives, we're not seeing the true picture are we? Does your picture need adjusting?

Panic attacks

As we've already seen, a panic (or anxiety) attack is a very common outcome of stress, and is the 'fight or flight' response in action. Your stomach may churn, heart race, breathing may be rapid, and you may sweat, feel faint, feel overwhelming fear and panic, and a sense of impending disaster, along with a pressing need to escape from the situation you find yourself in – a distressing and very frightening way to feel. Learning how to relax can be particularly helpful in learning how to deal with panic.

This ancient 'fight or flight' response can be triggered by events, or even by something as transient and unsubstantial as a fleeting thought. 'What if I can't get this done in time?', 'What if I can't pay those bills?' This response provides us with increased supplies of energy and muscle tone to help us to either run away from or fight whatever is endangering us. As already described, this is a very primitive but essential part of us, which developed as a primitive self-preservation response to physical danger. If we had to take the time to work out what to do when a sabre-toothed tiger or a speeding car suddenly bears down on us while crossing the street, it would already be too late. The 'fight or flight' reaction does it for us before we have time to think. For some, they can experience another common animal reaction to fear, and that is to freeze. Some people find themselves rooted to the spot, completely unable to move. That's why sometimes 'fight or flight' is referred to as 'fight, flight or freeze'.

But as we have seen, this reaction is just as easily brought into play in today's high-speed world by psychological danger. In other words, when there is danger to us as a person. For example, when we fear losing face, or not being able to cope, or being embarrassed in public, or if we feel out of control of our lives.

Case study – Kirsty

Kirsty walked into her doctor's consulting room, her face an unhappy mixture of fear and worry. She was 32, married and worked full time. Her eyes were downcast and she trembled as she slowly and hesitantly explained that she was sure she was going mad. Yesterday at work she had 'come over all peculiar'. She couldn't think straight, was convinced something terrible was about to happen, and her heart had pounded. She had also had a feeling of acute panic, and had found herself rushing out of the office without explaining. The funny thing was that as soon as she got home, she felt fine again. What was happening to her, she wondered. Was this a nervous breakdown? What would everyone think? What if it should happen again? Gentle questioning by her doctor revealed that she had been under pressure for some weeks as she was moving house, and had already bought a house, but couldn't sell her own. She wasn't sleeping well, and felt tired all the time.

A panic attack like this can be very frightening. It can feel like being the victim of a terrifying attack over which you appear to have absolutely no control. You can be convinced that you are going mad or are about to die. So what can you do if you have panic attacks?

COPING WITH PANIC ATTACKS

Anyone experiencing panic attacks, or even just feeling generally panicky, should work on doing the following four things. The first three make panic attacks much less likely to recur, and the fourth explains what to do if you have a panic attack.

1 *Firstly, the level of stress you experience can often be substantially reduced simply by understanding the bodily processes involved. This is even more true for panic attacks. Once the 'fight or flight' reaction is understood, the fantasy of an unpredictable and terrifying attack can be transformed into the reality of a completely natural automatic defence mechanism as described already. This can have a rapid and remarkable effect on people.*

Case study – Vera

I met a lady suffering from stress and panic attacks as she arrived at a seminar run by a local voluntary group. So unsteady was she that she required physical support to reach her seat to listen to an explanation of panic attacks being given by the speaker. She sat shaking at the back next to the door, hardly able to speak for anxiety. An hour later, at the end of the explanation, she was in the front row confidently asking questions.

2 *Secondly, reduce stress levels if at all possible, by removing the cause entirely, or reducing its effects in some way. Much more on how to do this is in the next chapter.*
3 *Thirdly, cushion yourself from the stress as much as possible using any of the relaxation techniques discussed in this book.*

4   *And lastly, learn to notice the first signs of a panic attack
    beginning, and use a quick relaxation or breathing technique
    at that point, as this will inhibit and possibly prevent the panic
    attack progressing any further. As the panic response is an
    automatic process, like breathing, simply telling your body not
    to panic will not be effective. Physical relaxation techniques,
    on the other hand, can reach behind the automatic response,
    allowing the brain to realize that the danger is subsiding,
    and begin to press the 'no need to panic' button. The PAUSE
    routine describes clearly how to do this.*

Try this – PAUSE routine

If you have a panic attack, or begin to feel panicky, the key is
to catch this early, and stop it in its tracks. This puts you back
in control. Here is one way of doing this. Don't be put off if
this method doesn't work the first or even the second time you
try it. Keep at it – it can be very effective:

1   *Work out what are your own first signs of a panic attack.
    This might be a lurch in the stomach, a thought in your
    mind, heart rate rising, or something else you've noticed.*
2   *Look out for these first signs, and when you notice them,
    you should immediately:*
    ▷ Pause... *and make yourself comfortable (sit down, lean
      on something etc.).*
    ▷ Absorb... *the detail of what's going on around you.*
    ▷ Use... *any method of relaxing quickly which works well
      for you, then*
    ▷ Slowly... *when you feel better,*
    ▷ Ease... *yourself back into what you were doing.*

The next chapter will show you the most effective ways to deal
with tension and stress, or to cushion yourself from future stresses
and strains, so that you are as resilient to these as you can be. You
will learn how to do this using a variety of relaxation techniques,
and also by using some other very useful practical strategies.

KEY POINTS

Look back over this chapter and choose the SIX pieces of information you found to be most interesting or helpful. Write these here, or go back and underline or highlight them in some way.

1 ....

2 ....

3 ....

4 ....

5 ....

6 ....

Look back over this chapter and choose the TWO practical suggestions you found to be most useful. Write these here, or go back and underline or highlight them in some way.

1 ....

2 ....

Look back over this chapter and choose TWO pieces of information you found to be surprising. Write these here, or go back and underline or highlight them in some way.

1 ....

2 ....

3

Coping with stress and tension

In this chapter you will learn:
- *how relaxation works*
- *more techniques for relaxing*
- *lots of ways to cushion yourself from stress*
- *about coping with stress.*

Formal stress management is thought to date back to World War I, 1914–18, during which many soldiers suffered from 'shell shock'. This was then assumed to be a neurological dysfunction resulting from brain damage caused by the sound of exploding shells. However, during World War II, 1939–45, this condition came to be thought of as an emotional breakdown caused by the 'stress' of combat, and was described as 'battle fatigue' or 'war neurosis'.

After 1945, there was a growing realization that many situations in everyday life could also provoke similar effects to battle fatigue. This, teamed with an interest by the military in training recruits to manage stress, and a new emphasis on personal development, gave rise to the introduction of stress management.

And of course, more recently, increasing attention has been paid to the true nature of battle fatigue, now termed post-traumatic stress disorder, or PTSD, which is now recognized to occur not just in response to battle, but to a wide range of traumatic events, such as accidents, disasters or abuse. PTSD is a very specific condition, and is not the same as the stress and tension caused by more 'everyday' situations.

Though we expect instant cures and magic new medications for every condition these days, sadly, there really is no instant magic wand yet for tension and stress. Dealing with stress does need effort, and does need time. But with a bit of know-how added to these, there is so much that can be done. So what this chapter will do is describe straightforward but effective ways to ease these problems, all with sound research to back them up. The first and most important of these is regular relaxation.

Slow down and make time for relaxation

As explained already, there are all sorts of ways to relax. It's down to personal preferences. The important thing is that the body is allowed to slow down and completely relax at least once every day. This could be for ten minutes, or it could be for an hour. A lazy bath, a walk, visiting friends, listening to music, yoga, sport, and so on, are all effective. Special relaxation techniques can also be useful because these can more easily be fitted into a busy day. These involve a bit of learning, but once you've practised them a few times, it all comes very easily. Relaxation like this can provide a regular relaxing break, and can help you to cope better with difficult situations.

If time is tight, it may seem that taking time to relax will just get you even further behind, but this isn't how it works. If your body is allowed to relax regularly, you will actually be able to get more done, more effectively with the remaining time, because you are refreshed, revived and energized.

THINK ABOUT YOUR BREATHING

If you are learning to relax, the best place to start is with your breathing. Breathing techniques are a common way to relax.

Here is a simple technique to help you to slow and regulate your breathing, and feel more relaxed, yet still remain alert enough to get on with your day.

Try this – 1-2-3 breathing

1 *Lie or sit comfortably, with good support.*
2 *Breathe out slowly, then take a gentle breath in to your own slow silent count of 1... 2... 3... then breathe out in your own time, again to your own slow and silent count of 1... 2... 3...*
3 *Continue gently breathing to this rhythm for a minute or two.*
4 *With practice, you will be able to leave out the counting, and just go into this rhythm when you need to.*

RELAX YOUR MIND AND THINKING

Sometimes the most difficult area to relax successfully is the mind itself, the thinking processes. These can be churning away, going over and over things, despite attempts to relax the body. Here is a way of tackling this.

Try this – Relaxing the mind

1 *Slow down and relax your body.*
2 *Once relaxed, picture as clearly as you can, or focus your mind on any one of these:*
  ▷ *waves lapping on the seashore*
  ▷ *branches swaying in the breeze*
  ▷ *deep dark green velvet*
  ▷ *a word or phrase such as 'peace', 'calm', 'relax'*
  ▷ *a calming poem, prayer or picture.*

Though relaxation is the main technique to use to cushion yourself from stress and tension, there are many other ways to approach this. They are not complicated, so it's not difficult to get a feel for what's involved. There are a number of general areas that can be addressed, such as taking breaks, managing time, lifestyle habits, exercise, thinking habits, assertiveness, setting priorities, and social support structure. If workplace stress is involved, all of these still apply, along with some other more specific additional strategies.

TAKING BREAKS AND MANAGING TIME

This one may sound obvious, but when you are run off your feet, and can't see a way out, or you feel you are indispensable, taking a break can seem impossible. Many people are working through their lunch break these days, and not taking all of their annual leave. It is, however, absolutely essential to have down-time, especially in these circumstances. It's all about not aiming too high to begin with, and about managing time more effectively.

Try this – Managing your time

▶ *Take regular breaks, especially from a stressful situation – even a five-minute break in a stressful morning can work wonders.*
▶ *Have a break for lunch.*
▶ *Plan and schedule breaks and holidays well ahead, so they are in your diary.*
▶ *Make time for yourself, and for hobbies, interests and leisure pursuits; this takes your mind off your troubles, and helps to keep them in perspective.*
▶ *If you have too much time on your hands, get involved in a hobby or voluntary activity, preferably with other people.*
▶ *Regularly do things you enjoy.*
▶ *Keep lists of jobs to be done, separating urgent and non-urgent.*
▶ *Select and prioritize what you do – you can't do it all.*
▶ *Plan your days and weeks in advance and keep a diary.*
▶ *Be organized and know where everything is.*
▶ *Accept that you cannot do everything.*
▶ *Work on the most demanding tasks when you are most refreshed.*
▶ *Remember that you need time for making decisions, for planning and for preparations.*
▶ *Do one job at a time.*
▶ *Delegate whenever possible.*

Exercise and lifestyle

Serotonin is a chemical that helps maintain a 'happy feeling', and seems to help keep our moods under control. It is sometimes referred to as a chemical messenger, or 'neurotransmitter', because when the brain produces serotonin a message is sent to the body and tension is eased.

The most effective way to raise serotonin levels naturally is with vigorous exercise. Studies have shown that serotonin levels are raised with increased activity, and the production of serotonin is increased for some days after the activity. Serotonin may also play a part in the 'runner's high', that feel-good buzz experienced by many runners.

Here are some thoughts on the benefits of building exercise into your life:

▶ *Regular physical activity which you enjoy and which fits in with your lifestyle is a very good general, everyday cushion for stress.*
▶ *There is a feel-good feeling both during and after exercise.*
▶ *After exercise it is much easier to relax.*
▶ *Try jogging, tennis, swimming, dancing of all kinds, rugby, judo, hill-walking, gardening, football, the gym, fitness videos, aerobics, and so on. Whatever you enjoy doing.*
▶ *Walking is generally all right for most people, but if you're unsure about beginning or resuming a particular form of exercise, check with your doctor first.*

Here are some general tips about how small changes in lifestyle can bring about marked improvements in stress and tension levels. Consider those which you could try to adopt, however, don't try to make too many changes all at once. This is too difficult. Make changes one at a time if you want them to last.

▶ *Eat a healthy and well-balanced diet that's low in fat, low in salt, high in fibre, and low in sugar, with five portions of fruit or vegetables every day, preferably with a variety of colours.*

- ▸ *Don't skip meals, especially breakfast and lunch.*
- ▸ *Eat regularly – no gaps longer than two to three hours – little and often is best.*
- ▸ *Avoid too much food or drink containing caffeine e.g. cola, coffee, chocolate. Having these occasionally is OK.*
- ▸ *Carbohydrates in the diet are important for serotonin production and because they trigger the release of insulin into the bloodstream. Insulin clears all the amino acids from the blood, except tryptophan. With the other amino acids out of the way, tryptophan can flood the brain, where it's converted to serotonin. Healthy carbohydrate-rich foods include wholegrain breads and crackers, wholegrain pasta, rice, cereal and fruit.*
- ▸ *Don't get into the habit of using alcohol or other substances to help you sleep or relax. You will build up a tolerance to these, so you will gradually need more and more to help you to relax or sleep.*
- ▸ *Get plenty of restful sleep – use relaxation or breathing techniques if you can't get off to sleep, or you wake up during the night.*

Insight

Many people switch off a little when exercise is mentioned. You hear so much about it. But exercise has a huge impact on tension. It's one of the most effective ways to feel more content in your skin, and more physically relaxed.

Thinking style

This may sound strange, but being aware of some of the ways that you think can make a real difference. And once you're aware of it, you're halfway to changing it. We all know people who seem to be able to cope with anything. The difference is usually in their attitude to life. Here are some ideas to think about. Much more on this in Chapter 7.

Which of the following might help you?

Avoid negative thinking:

▶ *Don't ignore the ordinary or good things that happen each day as if they don't count for some reason. Take account of the bad side of life, but don't dwell on it.*

▶ *When things go wrong it's not always your fault. Other people or the situation itself are just as often to blame.*

▶ *Take your mind off your problems as much as you can. They grow bigger the more you concentrate on them.*

Avoid 'should', 'ought' and 'must' thinking:

▶ *Do you often find yourself using one of these words, 'I must do this', 'I ought to do that', and so on?*

▶ *Ask yourself who is setting these personal standards and targets, and whether you are setting them too high.*

▶ *Let yourself off the hook, and lower these standards if necessary.*

HOW ASSERTIVE ARE YOU?

Communicating with, and relating to, others is always going to have its problems, stresses and strains. But behaving assertively, whenever possible, will help to ease that strain. Assertiveness is often confused with being aggressive, selfish and self-centred. This is just not the case. Assertiveness is really all about:

▶ *having respect for yourself and for others*
▶ *every human being having equal rights*
▶ *knowing and expressing your needs*
▶ *allowing others to express their needs, and hearing them*
▶ *being able to compromise with others.*

Everyone's behaviour will vary from situation to situation, but if a lot of what we do is not assertive, this can cause stress. When we are not assertive we are likely to be either manipulative, aggressive or passively giving in to others.

Try this – Assertiveness questionnaire

Completing this short questionnaire should give you a rough guide to how assertive you are.

Don't think too long about your answers. Your first response is usually the most accurate.

Rate whether you agree or disagree with each statement on a scale of 1–7, and enter the number in column 1.

1 = strongly agree
2 = moderately agree
3 = slightly agree
4 = neither agree nor disagree
5 = slightly disagree
6 = moderately disagree
7 = strongly disagree

Statement	Column 1	Column 2
I have difficulty saying 'no' to people.		
I often give in to other people's wishes and set aside my own.		
I find being criticized difficult.		
I am prone to aggressive outbursts.		
I feel much better about myself if I please other people.		
I find saying what I really think difficult.		
I often think other people are more important than I am.		
I say 'I'm sorry' a lot.		

(Contd)

Statement	Column 1	Column 2
I often get my way by making others feel guilty.		
I find speaking up in a group difficult.		
Total score		

Now total up your score, as a very basic form of assertiveness rating. As a very rough guide, scores of 60–70 indicate that you are almost always assertive, 50–59 that you are assertive most of the time, 40–49 that you are assertive some of the time, 20–39 that you are assertive occasionally, 0–19 that you are hardly ever or never assertive.

Now choose someone you know well – a friend, a partner, or a colleague perhaps – don't write down their name – and repeat the questionnaire rating them in your view, for each statement, in Column 2. Total it up. This may or may not reveal interesting differences!

BECOMING MORE ASSERTIVE

Here are some suggestions for becoming more assertive if you think that would be useful, but remember to take this slowly, and try out one new thing at a time. If you find these ideas particularly helpful, think about enrolling for a full course, or read up on the subject:

Saying 'no':

▶ *Keep it short, and say it confidently and warmly.*
▶ *Don't over-apologize.*
▶ *Ask for time to decide if you need it.*
▶ *Only give a reason if you feel you want to.*
▶ *Use a simple phrase you're comfortable with, such as 'I don't want to', or 'I'd rather not', 'Can't manage it today'.*
▶ *Calmly repeat your 'no' if the first one is not accepted.*

Remember you have the right to:

▶ *make a mistake*
▶ *have your own point of view*
▶ *fail if you try something*
▶ *try again*
▶ *expect others to listen to you.*

Other tips:

▶ *Value yourself.*
▶ *Value other people.*
▶ *Work out what you need and want out of life.*
▶ *Be prepared to compromise.*
▶ *Keep to any point you're making – don't let others distract you from it.*
▶ *Keep your voice slow, steady and low-pitched, and stay relaxed.*
▶ *Get your feeling of self-worth from within yourself, not just from other people.*

Insight

I'm always amazed at how many people think being assertive means being aggressive. And yet these are two very different ways to behave. I've always wondered how that mix-up came about. What do you think?

Sorting out your priorities

If you are being pulled in too many directions at one time, it pays to sort out your priorities. Time spent on this is time well spent. Without prioritizing, we would soon be overwhelmed and out of control, both of which often underlie stress. This operates at many levels: from the big picture of where you are going in life, through managing your weekly or monthly workload, to making sure the car is serviced today or this afternoon's dental appointment is not forgotten. At each level, prioritizing makes for a calmer, more smooth-running and relaxed day; it also brings satisfaction, a sense of achievement and a feeling of control.

Dr David Lewis describes how to work out your priorities based on deciding how urgent, and how important they are.

Priority	Urgent?	Important?
High	Yes	Yes
Medium	Yes	No
	No	Yes
Low	No	No

Done properly, prioritizing should also ensure that there is 'me-time' built in to your life. This is a top priority. No need to be selfish, just make sure you are looking after yourself too. Me-time is needed every day if you want to be relaxed every day. Here are some ideas on how to achieve this. You will find some overlap with the earlier discussion about time management, as these two processes are closely bound together. Adapt these to suit your situation, your personality and your preferences:

▶ *Take some time out to plan – days, weeks and months ahead.*
▶ *Set goals which are sensible and achievable.*
▶ *Listen to your inner voice when sorting out what's important to you, and what's not. Sort out what needs doing now, what can wait a bit, what could be done adequately by someone else (delegate), and what needn't be done at all. How important? How urgent?*
▶ *Take a few minutes each morning to check where you are with things.*
▶ *Use diaries, lists, stickies, reminder systems of all kinds – they sound boring, but they are all really useful.*
▶ *Don't rely on your memory, or on someone else's.*
▶ *Don't overdo the multitasking – it can produce chaos.*
▶ *It's OK to put some things off till tomorrow – just make sure they are the right things, and that you still get them done.*

- *Don't accept invitations or work which you know full well you can't manage.*
- *Going away, taking a break and coming back to something can help to get it all into perspective. This can be for five minutes, an hour, a weekend, or a week in the sun.*

LEISURE

Taking part in some sort of leisure activity regularly, as well as having other interests and activities outside the regular work and chores routine, can act as very effective cushioning against stress. Leisure pursuits can also provide support through the friendships they can bring, and reduce tension and stress by giving you a break. If, on the other hand, you have too much time available, a hobby or pastime can give you something to do, or provide a new challenge if you need one. We all need a bit of a challenge in our lives. Leisure pursuits can also help to prevent an individual's identity and self-image relying entirely on their job. Working on using, improving and developing these areas of your life can have quite an impact on how you feel.

Insight

It seems to me that having breaks and leisure time is often overlooked as a way of relaxing by busy, tense people. It's as if they feel that they just don't have the time, so there's nothing they can do to reduce their tension. But it's a kind of chicken and egg, or cart and horse question. If you can deliberately make time for breaks and leisure, you will actually find that you feel much better, have more energy, and can get things done more quickly and more efficiently. Worth a try, surely?

Cushioning yourself and feeling good

Build a routine for yourself so that the following things happen every week without your having to plan them.

Cushion	How often	Suggestions
Relaxation – body	Every day	Any technique Any relaxing physical activity
Relaxation – mind	Every day	Any technique Pastime which occupies the mind
Breathing skills	Every day	Any technique
Exercise	30 mins of moderate-intensity activity, five days a week, OR 20 mins of high-intensity activity, three days a week (older adults recommended to use moderate-intensity level)	Walking Swimming Dancing Running Exercise machine Whatever you enjoy – may also double as a form of relaxation, leisure pursuit or hobby
Leisure	At least once or twice weekly	Whatever you enjoy doing – may also double as a form of relaxation or exercise

Hobby/Pastime	At least once or twice weekly	Whatever you enjoy doing – may also double as a form of relaxation or exercise
Breaks	Every day, every week, every few months	Whatever and whenever you prefer
Diet	Every day	Healthy diet Avoid caffeine Eat breakfast Avoid long gaps between food Avoid sugar
Thinking	Every day	Accentuate the positive Talk positively Mix with positive people Be nice to yourself Avoid negative people Avoid 'must', 'ought' and 'should'
Assertiveness	Every day	Say 'no' when you should Look after your needs too
Support	Regularly	Share your problems and experiences with someone supportive that you can trust

A PROBLEM SHARED

All of us need someone who cares about us and who is interested in what we do. This can bring relief from existing stress, and can even prevent us from feeling stressed in the first place. A problem shared really is a problem halved. Research bears this out, and reinforces the importance of having social support of some kind. You can get this important support from a number of places:

▶ *family, friends or partner*
▶ *at work from colleagues or clients*
▶ *from groups you belong to (Internet included)*
▶ *from supportive groups or individuals in your community.*

It is no sign of weakness to seek such support. Human beings naturally group together, and this can be really effective. However, you need to be careful only to confide in those you can trust.

Insight

I've known countless people who have looked visibly better, with a noticeable change in appearance and body language, immediately after having talked out their problems and worries with someone they trust. No major solutions produced, they simply feel a huge release of tension from having got their 'story' out.

Work stress

Stress caused by work is particularly common today. Employers are becoming increasingly aware of this and some are offering training or even counselling to help staff cope with stress. The list of causes would be endless, and most are not easily tackled by the employee themselves, or the self-employed.

Consider which apply to you:

- *long hours*
- *being overloaded*
- *tight deadlines*
- *difficult people*
- *job insecurity*
- *juggling family and job*
- *incompetence in others*
- *working conditions*
- *isolation*
- *conflict with others*
- *role uncertainty*
- *being a workaholic*
- *business problems*
- *bullying*
- *constant change*
- *low pay*
- *shift work*
- *travel to work*
- *demands on home life*
- *always on duty*
- *the responsibility*
- *moving home a lot*
- *poor communication*
- *being away from home a lot*
- *unlikely promotion*
- *lack of confidence*
- *lack of control*
- *noise/heat/cold.*

Often, the actual cause of stress at work is difficult to tackle, so the most common way to deal with work stress is to cushion yourself from it in the ways already described. Relaxation, breaks, social support, a healthy lifestyle, and leisure activities all have a part to play. Think very carefully before you tackle a problem head-on at work. Remember, there may be repercussions for your job or future career.

Recent changes in working conditions and methods have often meant that people unaccustomed to it are having to speak up in meetings, give presentations, or to work in teams. This often means that a job which was previously no problem for an individual, can easily become a stressful one, often without much warning or training being given.

Here are some other general pointers to think about:

- *Are you a square peg in a round hole? Does your personality not really suit the job? If so, and you can change your job, this may be a solution. If you can't, cushioning is the best answer.*
- *Perhaps you have a low tolerance for stress. Many people do. If so, can you find a less stressful job? If not, cushioning is again the best solution.*
- *Would learning some new skills make a difference? What about assertiveness, confidence building, time management, team working, delegation, new technology? Are courses like this available to you either at work, or from adult education?*
- *Is confidential counselling available at work? Some employers now provide this entirely separately and independent of the workplace.*

> **Insight**
> When you wake each morning think of one thing, no matter how small, you can do that day to improve your life, or even someone else's.

What about medication?

The consequences of stress and tension tend to be physical and emotional symptoms which make us feel ill, and when we are ill most people consult a doctor. Many doctors will provide a combination of medication and advice. In some GP practices, you might be referred for counselling or other talking therapy, though waiting times and availability vary.

The drugs used by doctors in the treatment of stress and tension have usually been effective, though up until now many have had unfortunate side effects which made them unsuitable for long-term use. Initially opiates were used because of their mood-altering and pain-relieving properties. Laudanum, or tincture of opium, was widely used. Regrettably, it had the property of inducing sleep which may have been welcome to some, but it was and is also very addictive, which is less welcome.

It is perhaps not surprising that when benzodiazepines were invented they were widely welcomed for their ability to physically relax stressed or tense patients. The best-known benzodiazepine is Valium (diazepam). Valium is still widely used and, like many forms of treatment, if used properly it can be very effective, but not perhaps best as a treatment for stress. It can be used to relieve tension in the short term, but is best not used over long periods, as it tends to need a higher dosage to get the same effect after a few months. It was the arrival of a drug called Ativan which really changed things. Ativan, unlike Valium, was short acting and quickly lost its effect, requiring a further dose, making it very addictive and quickly giving benzodiazepines as a class of drug a bad reputation.

Most people have heard of Prozac (fluoxetine). Prozac is an antidepressant of a completely new type, the first of a class of drugs known as selective serotonin re-uptake inhibitors (SSRI), which alter the way the brain deals with the products of noradrenalin. Cipramil (citalopram) and Seroxat (paroxetine) soon followed, bringing relief to many patients who suffer from depression. It was soon realized that these drugs also reduce anxiety, and Seroxat was given a licence for anxiety and panic disorder, both of which can occur in stressed patients. Prozac and Cipramil share this effect and all three are prescribed for these qualities. They can have potential side effects, but if properly used together with appropriate advice they can be of great benefit for tension and stress. A non-sedating way to control some of the effects of stress, particularly on the heart, is to use 'beta blockers'. These block the 'beta' or cardiac effects of adrenalin, the stress hormone. They slow and regulate the heart and stop palpitations, inducing a feeling of calmness.

KEY POINTS

Look back over this chapter and choose the TWO pieces of information you found to be most interesting or helpful. Write these here, or go back and underline or highlight them in some way.

1 ....

2 ....

Look back over this chapter and choose the FOUR practical suggestions you found to be most useful. Write these here, or go back and underline or highlight them in some way.

1 ....

2 ....

3 ....

4 ....

Which TWO techniques or suggestions from this chapter would you like to try out straight away?

Write these here, or go back and underline or highlight them in some way.

1 ....

2 ....

Which TWO techniques or suggestions from this chapter would you like to work towards using regularly?

(Contd)

Write these here, or go back and underline or highlight them in some way.

1 ....

2 ....

4

....

Vulnerability to tension or stress

In this chapter you will learn:
- *how personality may be linked to tension and stress*
- *that your body may be very reactive to stress*
- *how your coping strategies can make things worse*
- *the link between control and stress.*

Most people, at some point in their lives, will come up against life or workplace stress, and they may find themselves with upsetting and worrying symptoms of some kind. George, who is 54 and has been unemployed for three years, now has irritable bowel syndrome. Then there's Sally, a single mother of three small children from a deprived area, who is underweight and has frequent tension headaches. Then we have Dev, a young very over-worked executive who just can't sleep, and is exhausted. It is easy to imagine how George, Sally and Dev feel, and to understand why they are having problems.

But we also all probably know other people who have coped with similar situations without experiencing any stress or symptoms at all. Or those who crumble at the slightest difficulty. What is the difference? Are some people more vulnerable to stress than others? Are they weaker people? The simple answers are that yes, some people are more vulnerable to stress in certain circumstances, but no, they certainly are not weaker people.

Hot spots

Tension or stress can be a problem for anyone. Even those who believe they thrive on stress, are strong enough to withstand whatever is thrown at them and are immune to all that, in certain circumstances, or due to just one event, will find themselves in difficulties. Everyone appears to have their own particular vulnerabilities, and their own particular 'hot spots'. This chapter will explain more about this.

Most people are vulnerable to stress, through no fault of their own. Here are some reasons why you might be more likely to experience tension and stress. Consider which 'hot spots' apply to you:

▶ *easily startled*
▶ *highly strung*
▶ *not much support from family or friends*
▶ *cope with stress by working through breaks*
▶ *had a bereavement in the last 12 months*
▶ *lacking in confidence*
▶ *lost something important to you in the last 12 months*
▶ *react quickly to events*
▶ *blame yourself when things go wrong*
▶ *relationship broke up in the last 12 months*
▶ *cope with stress by working through all or part of your holidays*
▶ *tend to be overly emotional*
▶ *cope with stress by doing things faster*
▶ *lack a sense of challenge in life*
▶ *serious illness or medical procedure in the last 12 months*
▶ *have already had very difficult life events*

- *frequent minor ailments in the last 12 months*
- *anxiety or nervousness in one or more close family members*
- *feeling you have no control over your life*
- *lost your job in the last 12 months*
- *lack a sense of commitment in life*
- *about to lose your job*
- *cope with stress by working longer hours*
- *moved house recently.*

For some people, the automatic or 'autonomic' arousal of their nervous system, brought on by stress, does happen more easily because of their constitutional make-up. They have a 'labile' or 'over-reactive' autonomic nervous system, and are easily startled. They clearly have no control over this, and can no more be blamed for it than for having brown hair, long fingers, or green eyes. In fact, they would have been the survivors in prehistoric life when physical threat was frequent, and may even have been admired greatly for their lightning reaction to danger. This is quite likely to have been inherited, so close relatives may have similar problems too.

So, there are major differences between people in terms of the physiology they were born with, as well as the circumstances surrounding the here and now and the past 12 months or so. There are also wide differences between people in four other areas:

- *personality*
- *previous experiences*
- *ways of coping with stress*
- *the sort of social support they have (if any).*

Again, people have little or no choice or control over these factors, but each of these can increase or decrease your vulnerability to stress in certain circumstances.

But the picture is not a simple one. There isn't a clear set of these personal characteristics which is more likely to encourage stress than any other. Nor is there any in-built problem or weakness attached to any particular characteristic. It really all depends on the particular mix of person and situation.

In our world, there are many, many ways of living, and many different cultures and lifestyles. Though globalization is making life anywhere in the world more and more similar, there are still huge variations between life in, say, Africa or China and North America or the UK. Even within each country, lifestyles and culture can be varied and diverse. What happens in any particular culture or way of life is that some characteristics will tend to make life easier to cope with, but others will tend to increase vulnerability to stress.

Let's look at some examples. Take the perfectionist. In many aspects of life in the UK today, the person with this characteristic has a high likelihood of being vulnerable to stress. The perfectionist working in a job such as social work, teaching, or police work may find themselves stressed because they can't deal with everything perfectly and as they would like. These are jobs which often require prioritizing and limiting the amount of work that can be tackled due to restraints of time and resources. There are many other jobs with similar problems. The in-tray is never empty. The loose ends are never tied up. On the other hand, all things being equal, the perfectionist working as a pharmacist or radiologist, where performance must be as complete and mistake-free as possible, is much more likely to be stress free.

There is also now evidence to suggest that being part of a social network provides protection against stressful life events, and against stress-related ill health. This social support can come from family, friends, work colleagues or the local community. The more varied and extensive the support the better. Those with little support of this kind are therefore vulnerable to stress, and can find coping with the daily hassles and problems of life difficult.

But no one is immune to stress. No matter what your constitutional make-up, your personality characteristics, coping style, your social support or your previous experience, there will still be situations which can bring about stress. We all have our 'hot spots' or 'stress buttons' which can be pressed to bring about stress.

We now turn to look in more detail at those factors, other than our in-born constitution and social support, which can contribute to individual vulnerability. We'll focus on personality, previous experience and coping style. The information presented may be useful for you to assess your own personal vulnerability to stress.

Insight

I'm often surprised how many people feel they don't have a choice. And they feel so weighed down by this. But we do have a choice in everything in life. And we also have a right to make that choice.

Personality

Tempora mutantur, et nos mutamur in illis.
(Times change, and we change with them.)

Latin, Emperor Lothar I, 795–855

Even today, the argument still continues about whether our personality is constant and stable, or whether it can change. But people can and certainly do show different aspects of their personality in different situations. How many men have to be the doting father one minute, authoritarian manager the next and an indulgent lover the next? And do people not change over time? Angry, moody and stubborn at 18, full of initiative, drive and urgency at 35, cautious, methodical and concerned about the environment at 55.

Arguments can be made both for this kind of changing personality with the situation and over time, and also for more permanence in our general disposition. But if we spend too much time on this ongoing argument, there will be no opportunity to explain the undoubted link between certain personality characteristics and stress. So, in order to simplify matters, let us assume for the moment that in a given situation at some point in time an individual behaves and thinks in accordance with certain fairly constant personality traits, and that this will affect their experience of stress.

TYPE A AND TYPE B PERSONALITIES

Probably the best-known model linking personality and stress was developed by two cardiologists, Dr Meyer Friedman and Dr Ray Rosenman in 1974. They described two extremes of personality and thinking style described as Type A and Type B. Type A is prone to stress, and it is suggested that over time this type of behaviour can lead to premature coronary artery disease. On the other hand, Type B is less stress prone, and therefore less likely to succumb to stress-related illness. Take these two examples of behaviour and thinking.

Case study

Yolanda

Yolanda is 34 and manager of a small but growing electronics firm. She jumps out of bed in the morning as soon as the alarm goes off, eats toast and drinks strong black coffee at the same time as reading some papers from work, before grabbing her briefcase and the other paperwork she was working on last night and dashing off to the car.

It doesn't start first time, so she mutters angrily about how she never has time to arrange its service. She has barely allowed time to get to work before the first of numerous important meetings. Today of all days, if this meeting goes well, it could mean a very important deal clinched. Mercifully the car then purrs into life, and she heaves a sigh of relief and sets off.

But within minutes she has hit roadworks and slow-moving traffic, and another car pulls in sharply in front of her. 'Stupid fool' she barks, banging on the horn. Her anger rises and so does her heart rate. She sighs again. Where has this traffic come from unexpectedly? Why didn't she leave earlier? Tension persists and increases throughout her body; she grips the wheel tightly, and turns up the volume of the music on the radio.

She reaches work late, and bellows at her secretary to get her a coffee, and why hadn't she called to warn her about the roadworks?

Lee

Lee is 37 and manages a small but growing knitwear factory. He wakes to the sound of relaxing music on his radio, and gets up slowly and stretches. Important meeting on today, so he's allowed extra time to get to work in case of traffic. After sitting down to breakfast and a chat with his wife, he glances through the business pages of the paper then walks out to the car, noticing the roses could do with a prune as he passes them. The car has just had its regular service and bursts into life at the first turn of the key. Soon he hits single-line traffic, starting when the car alongside of him suddenly pulls in before him. He assumes the driver must be in a hurry to get somewhere, then forgets about it. On arriving at work, he has time to look over the day's appointments before his secretary arrives.

These are, of course, people at the two extremes, Yolanda being a Type A and Lee a Type B. But the different styles of thinking and behaving clearly have repercussions, and scenes such as these will be re-enacted in countless homes, offices, schools and factories every day.

The belief system and behaviour of Type A people increases their vulnerability to stress. They find it hard to relax without feeling guilty, their self-worth is bound up with their achievements and they are therefore compelled towards success and accomplishment in everything they do. Anything that delays these goals therefore incurs frustration and anger. There are no allowances made for mistakes, or for flexibility. This produces frequent autonomic arousal due to a hectic pace and persistent appraisal of threat, which is undiminished by breaks for relaxation of any kind.

Rather than being at these two extremes, most individuals will actually show a mixture of Type A and Type B behaviour. Where do you think you fit in?

The following behaviours are typical of Type A and can help to identify it. Consider which apply to you:

- *doing everything quickly – talking, eating, walking*
- *impatience, especially in queues*
- *strongly competitive*
- *not planning time realistically – self-imposed deadlines which are too tight*
- *emphasizing key words in their normal speech*
- *being unable to relax or do nothing without a sense of guilt*
- *hurrying other people's speech by finishing their sentences for them*
- *frequently doing two or more things at once*
- *working towards poorly defined goals*
- *becoming oblivious to beauty and things of interest around them*
- *material success is very important*
- *a chronic sense of time urgency, and arranging more and more into less and less time*
- *hostility and aggression, especially to other Type A personalities*
- *using gestures such as a clenched fist, or banging on the table for emphasis.*

Rosenman and Friedman describe the following characteristics as typical of Type B. Consider which apply to you:

- *being free of Type A characteristics*
- *feeling no need to impress others with their achievements*
- *able to relax without feeling guilty*
- *no sense of time urgency*
- *no in-built hostility or competitiveness*

- *slow, calm and attentive*
- *warm, medium-volume voice.*

Since most people display a combination of Type A and Type B behaviours and thinking style, it is useful to be aware of how these might be contributing to the overall picture of someone's experience of stress.

Insight

A recent book featured a compilation of letters that celebrities would have written to themselves at age 16. An intriguing and revealing thing to do. Give this a try if you feel like it.

THE OBSESSIONAL PERSONALITY

Here we are not talking about the person who exhibits extreme behaviour and has a problem such as obsessional hand-washing or cleaning. No, many completely ordinary people have an element of obsessional behaviour within their personality which is not a sign of any kind of problem. For example, the perfectionist mentioned earlier could be thought of as showing mildly obsessive behaviour, being someone who cannot tolerate mistakes in themselves or even in others. Other obsessional individuals might set high standards for themselves and others in terms of punctuality, conscientiousness or conformity. Obsessionality is characterized by an inability to tolerate variations from their chosen way of doing things, or a chosen subject for sole consideration. Such individuals have very fixed thinking, and are strongly resistant to change and new ideas. They are most at home in a situation where everything is precise and predictable. So, if their environment does not comply with their particular obsessionality, stress will probably be the outcome.

Case study

Gita

Gita, 42 and currently single, is an office worker for a major bank. She keeps everything neat and tidy and in its place at all times.

(Contd)

She just cannot tolerate the slightest untidiness, or lack of organization. All is well, until a new office junior, Brian, starts work and refuses to comply with her wishes. He says he works better with a muddle around him. Gita now finds she is losing weight as she has lost her appetite, and her old migraine problem has recurred. She visits her GP complaining of stress at work.

Joseph

Joseph is the 50-year-old manager of a biscuit factory, and is used to an authoritarian system which has always allowed him to choose and put into place his own choice of production methods. But team-working has just been introduced into the company and the production methods are now to be decided by a team of which he is only one member. He finds it difficult to accept the views of others on how things should be done, and has recently felt tired all the time and has now begun to wake up with an anxiety attack during the night before team meetings. He complains to his wife that he is stressed at work.

So, two people complaining of workplace stress. Each with a very different problem, but both having an origin within themselves, rather than in the workplace.

THE 'HARDY' PERSONALITY

In 1979, Suzanne Kobasa, developed her theory of 'hardiness' with respect to the ability of an individual to withstand stress. After studying a group of executives who were experiencing similar high levels of stress, she found that certain personality characteristics made it less likely that the stress would result in mental or physical ill health. She asserted that this group of attributes comprised what she defined as a 'hardy' personality. These attributes, 'the three Cs', are:

- ▶ **Commitment** – *an active involvement in and commitment to a range of areas of life, such as work, family, friends and institutions.*

> ▶ **Control** – *a feeling of being in control of your life, and able to influence events.*
> ▶ **Challenge** – *an acceptance of change as inevitable, and being open and willing to try new things which are embraced as a challenge.*

So, those who have a sense of commitment, a feeling of control and enjoy change and new activities are less likely to experience stress. In contrast to this, those who have little personal commitment, feel a lack of control over their lives, and enjoy stability rather than change are vulnerable to stress. More recently, the term 'resilience' has been used to describe a similar concept. The idea of 'cushioning' introduced earlier in the book, aims to increase 'resilience' to stress.

It is probably fair to add that this scenario described by Kobasa, is going to be mainly relevant to a life in which change is common and frequent. So, in a society where there is constant unpredictable change, such as current Western society, the three Cs will provide stress-proofing, or increase resilience. But there is a huge variation in culture and lifestyle in the world, both now, and in the past. If times change and life becomes very predictable and unchanging, the whole situation might be very different.

A sense of control

Kobasa includes a sense of control in her hardy personality, and the whole idea of control seems to be a vital one in any discussion about stress. It seems intuitively correct that faced with a threatening or difficult situation over which we have no control, stress is likely to be that much greater than if we feel able to do something about it. But sometimes awareness of whether or not we have control is less clear-cut than we might think.

Case study

Simon

Simon has just begun a course in biochemistry at a large university, and is finding it increasingly difficult to cope with the work.

(Contd)

The lectures are complicated, and the pace is faster than he expected. It's difficult to get to know people as the lectures have so many people in them. He now feels, after only six weeks, that the work is totally out of his control and that he just isn't up to it. He's also been feeling panicky and light-headed during lectures, and has had to leave the lecture for some fresh air on several occasions. He's sure he'll have to give up at the end of the semester, and is angry that life isn't fair. Why do these things always happen to him?

Anya

Anya is on the same course as Simon and has noticed him having to go out of the room during lectures. She found the sudden increase in pace and level a shock at first, but decided she would need to put in more study to keep up, and that seemed to work. She also made a point of talking to other students, and discovered they all felt the same. She finds the library helpful to find books on the parts of the course she finds difficult to understand, and the tutorials are very useful for asking questions. She's confident she can cope with the course and is enjoying the experience.

As early as 1966, J. B. Rotter was describing the significance of people's perception of whether or not they have control over situations. He introduced the concept of 'locus of control', and would describe Simon as having an 'external locus of control', and Anya, an 'internal locus of control'. That is, Anya feels she has her own, internal control over what happens to her, and that her actions and decisions have an effect on her life experience. So she works harder, finds out how others are feeling and gets further help from the library. Simon, on the other hand, feels he has little influence or control over events, and that external factors such as fate or chance are largely responsible for what happens to him. So he sits back and takes whatever happens to him as if he has no power to alter it. A kind of 'learned helplessness'. Simon is therefore likely to experience stress, while Anya is not.

Attitudes

Confidence in oneself is only one example of a range of attitudes which we may have, and which may have been influenced and brought about by our previous experience. These will all have repercussions in making people vulnerable to stress. For example, people may have become:

- ▶ *particularly suspicious of others*
- ▶ *pessimistic*
- ▶ *prone to feelings of guilt*
- ▶ *withdrawn*
- ▶ *dependent on others*
- ▶ *hostile*
- ▶ *aggressive.*

All of these behaviours in the wrong place or at the wrong time can produce stress.

Insight

It seems to me that you can think things through, and weigh it all up, and look at the pros and cons, but sometimes, you just have to take a leap of faith, and let yourself go.

Previous experiences

An individual who has experienced a number of negative life events in childhood or in adulthood, is more likely to suffer stress again in the future. This is by no means a certainty, it's just that it's more likely than for the 'average' person. There are two reasons for this. First of all, David Barlow in 1988 suggested that previous experience of uncontrollable and/or unpredictable life events can result in constant apprehension even in the absence of a new stress. This is also a common outcome of intermittent stress, especially if we have no control over it. A neighbour who has a noisy, late-night party every few months would be an example of this kind of stressor. Secondly, any new stress is much more likely to trigger an exaggerated stress response, as the individual's autonomic system has now become sensitized to stress.

Let's move on now to consider the sorts of coping strategies we might use to deal with stress, and the surprising effects these can have.

> **Insight**
> People can sometimes feel like a 'prisoner of their life experiences'. But some of those prison bars are self-made. The secret is to find the self-made ones and break them or bend them, to let you escape.

Ways of coping with stress

Probably one of the most important aspects of people's previous experience is the coping strategies which they have learned to use when stressed. In the main these tend to be counter-productive and unhelpful. Knowing how to deal effectively with stress does not come naturally. It is during childhood and throughout life when we have to deal with stress that we develop strategies for coping with it.

Generally, we acquire these strategies by copying others, or by applying what we think is common sense, or using what we find works. If our parents reacted to stress by running about wringing their hands, or by bottling it all up, we may well do the same. After all, we learn how to tie our laces and to speak by copying the adults around us, so it's not surprising that we learn how to deal with stress in a similar way. We also learn ways of coping with stress from wider society. So, if people in general say that taking your mind off things is a useful thing to do, we are likely to give it a try, and if it works, this will become part of our repertoire for dealing with stress.

Having said all this, sometimes a strategy may not really be a conscious choice at all. Many people automatically speed up or keep busy in response to stress, probably due to the autonomic changes that are happening, mobilizing the body for physical action. Other strategies such as denial or blaming others may be equally unconscious, and these are likely to be largely the outcome of our psychological make-up.

Some of these coping strategies are helpful, some unhelpful. Some can even be helpful in some situations, unhelpful in others. But many people who are finding stress is getting on top of them are likely to be using coping strategies which are at best not helping, and at worst, may even be making matters worse.

It is useful to be aware of the kinds of unhelpful strategies people might use to cope with their stress. It is always helpful to take stock of these before more effective strategies are tried out. Let's take a closer look at some of these now.

UNHELPFUL COPING STRATEGIES

Increased substance use
Many people drink or smoke to excess, and this is often an outcome of even a low level of stress. The use of prescription and non-prescription drugs is also a common reaction to stress. Not only is this behaviour counter-productive in terms of stress, but the added risks to health are obvious.

Comfort eating
In childhood, it is common to learn to associate feeling relaxed and at ease with eating, and it's easy to see how that can happen with sweets used as rewards or to reduce the pain of a grazed knee. Comfort eating is therefore a frequent reaction to stress. This then creates its own health risks if your weight and sugar intake begin to increase as a result.

Working longer, harder and faster
If you have too much to do in too little time, whether paid or unpaid, this leads to stress. Many businesses and services have

'down-sized' to save on costs, but this has simply piled more work onto the remaining staff. An understandable and common reaction to having too much to do is to work harder and work longer hours, to get everything done, usually with fewer and shorter breaks. You might skip lunch, or have lunchtime meetings, work late, skip days off to catch up, take work home, miss out on holidays and so on. To add to the pressure, there may be no option as your job and livelihood, or your family's well-being may depend on getting through the workload. Nowadays, 'presentism' is becoming a problem at work, rather than 'absenteeism', with employers expecting their workforce to work longer hours to show commitment to the job. But all of these coping strategies will actually make matters worse. The body will rapidly become tired, drained and open to disease, and also become less resistant to stress. A vicious circle will ensue, whereby the individual will feel more stressed and will probably become physically and psychologically ill, while doing nothing to tackle the real problem.

Over-activity
Another common reaction to stress is to keep very busy with other things, sometimes to excess. You fill every minute of the day with work, hobbies, clubs, sport or socializing. This can be an outcome of physiological arousal, which can be experienced as the feeling that you simply can't stop, and that you have to keep going. On the other hand, this can be a way of avoiding the stressful situation. All of this activity usually means that the problem itself is being avoided and not dealt with, and arousal is being maintained over longer and longer periods. This has an exhausting effect.

Denial
There are various forms of denial, the majority of them harmful in most situations. The exception to this is temporary denial, which can be protective in the case of a serious trauma such as sexual abuse, rape or the death of a loved one. When in denial you may:

▶ *bottle everything up inside*
▶ *pretend it's not a problem*
▶ *reason it all away*

- *hide your feelings*
- *carry on as if nothing has happened*
- *put on a brave face.*

Denial is particularly likely if you see admitting to a problem with stress as a sign of weakness, which it is not. In any event, denial means the situation causing the stress is not being tackled, and in the long term this can mean exhaustion, stress-related illness, or sudden angry outbursts.

Escapism

It is common to simply escape from a problem situation rather than dealing with it. You might move from job to job, or from relationship to relationship, never attempting to sort out difficulties. This can make your life become a downward spiral, with no sense of roots or stability.

Taking it out on other people

This takes the form of either blaming others for everything, or taking out your feelings of anger and frustration on them. Your nearest and dearest will often be the main targets for this type of anger. Apart from relieving some of these pent-up emotions, little benefit is achieved by this, and much damage can be done to relationships.

So, many coping tactics only succeed in making matters worse. They may help in the very short term, but then just stoke up more stress. The coping tactic which has most effect on tension and stress is learning to relax, and then using this new skill every day. Sounds easy, but it requires motivation and dedication to stick with this. A good social support network can make this much easier. The next two chapters will explain physical relaxation and its history, and give you lots of ways of relaxing the body to try out, and see what works for you.

KEY POINTS

Look back over this chapter and choose the FIVE pieces of information you found to be most interesting or helpful. Write these here, or go back and underline or highlight them in some way.

1 ....

2 ....

3 ....

4 ....

5 ....

Look back over this chapter and choose the THREE practical suggestions you found to be most useful. Write these here, or go back and underline or highlight them in some way.

1 ....

2 ....

3 ....

Which TWO techniques or suggestions from this chapter would you like to work towards using regularly?

Write these here, or go back and underline or highlight them in some way.

1 ....

2 ....

5

Relaxing your body

In this chapter you will learn:
- *how tension affects your body and mind*
- *the difference simple changes in breathing can make*
- *lots of ways to relax*
- *ways to get a better night's sleep.*

Understanding helps you to relax

There is a well-known phrase, 'ignorance is bliss'. And so it may be in some circumstances and situations. However, it is most certainly not true of tension and relaxation. And I use the word 'ignorance' in its accurate meaning, that of a 'lack of knowledge', and not in its current more pejorative usage.

Not understanding what is happening to your body when you are tense can just add to the tension. This brings about a vicious circle, which can mean tension simply gets worse and worse over time, sometimes, quite rapidly. This is because tension can make you feel very strange. It can produce a range of unusual and disconcerting symptoms, such as shaking, moderate to severe pain, and light-headedness. All of these usually indicate to a person that something is wrong, and so this induces worry, or anxiety. This produces yet more tension, and so more symptoms, more worry, and so on. You can see how this can happen, creating a bigger and bigger problem as if out of nowhere.

But if a person can understand what is going on, as described in previous chapters, and know that what they are experiencing is a normal and harmless reaction, then this vicious circle can be prevented from being established, or will be unravelled if it has already been formed. And what relief this can bring. As we've seen, being able to relax well can be achieved using many, many practical techniques. But your skill will be enhanced in any of these through your understanding of what's happening to your body and your mind. It's easier then to simply let it happen. There's no need to have an intricate knowledge of the physiological details for this, just a nodding acquaintance with the broad brush strokes of this wonderful process is enough. That's what this book can provide.

Changes in breathing

But where to start? An essential process of just being alive is breathing, or respiration. And as such this is a fundamental process involved in tension and relaxation. One of the first signs of an increase in tension will be an increased breathing rate. Not necessarily noticeable, just an extra breath or two per minute. Barely perceptible, but this will affect the body's complex processes and chemistry substantially, especially if it goes on for a few minutes or longer, as it often does. Breathing like this can go on for hours at a time. Similarly, one of the first signs of a body relaxing, is the slowing down of the rate of respiration.

In many ways the most significant physical change which accompanies tension is the onset of inappropriate breathing. This was studied and explained by L. C. Lum of the Respiratory Physiology Unit of Papworth and Addenbrookes Hospital, Cambridge, in 1977. By inappropriate breathing, Lum meant hyperventilation. This is often described or acted out in films and cartoons as a kind of hysterical behaviour, with obvious gulping of air and rapid breathing. This can happen in extreme cases, but in most cases of tension, there is little to see outwardly. Everyday tension produces over-breathing. This means that people begin to breathe faster, and mainly using the upper chest. Nothing particularly noticeable to the casual observer, no hysteria, just a slight or moderate change in speed and style of breathing. Here are some of the most common signs of this type of breathing:

▶ *weakness*
▶ *tired all the time*
▶ *numbness or tingling in hands or feet, arms, legs or face*
▶ *trembling or twitching*
▶ *painful muscles*
▶ *poor concentration*
▶ *feeling panicky*
▶ *heart racing*
▶ *difficulty swallowing or getting your breath*
▶ *dizziness or light-headedness.*

Normal respiration is mainly abdominal with little effort being contributed by the muscles of the thorax (chest). It is regular, quiet and unobtrusive. Just watch a cat or a baby lying relaxed and asleep. They will breathe with their tummy muscles, not their chest. Their tummy will slowly and evenly rise and fall. This is the way we were designed to breathe.

Insight

Most of us have a world filled with deadlines, targets, schedules and priorities. If you identify with this, don't let it make you lose sight of what's really important in your life.

Try this – Breathing rate and stress

This activity is best completed in one sitting. You will need a watch or clock which will allow you to time 1–2 minutes, a pen or pencil, and two pieces of paper – have these ready before you begin. Sit down comfortably.

1 *How are you feeling at the moment? Without thinking too much about it, rate how positive you feel about life in general*
(Contd)

at this very moment on a scale of 1–100, 100 being the highest and most positive, and 1 being the lowest score. Write it down on one of the pieces of paper.

2 *As you are sitting there quietly, just count how many inward breaths you are taking in one minute. Write the number on the same piece of paper, under the first number. Now turn this paper over, or put it away, so that you can't see it for the remainder of the activity.*

3 *Now, on the second sheet of paper, list all the items in the news over the past few weeks or months that you can think of which you have found worrying – local, national or international – **but allow yourself only one minute to do this.***

4 *Now, below this, explain and describe in detail an incident which has made you feel really stressed at some point in your life. This could be anything at all – work, family, finances, whatever you can think of. Explain as much as you can about what happened and about how it made you feel – **but allow yourself only one minute to complete this.***
  (If you are lucky enough to have had no stresses, or would rather not write about a stressful incident, write down a list of events or circumstances which you feel would stress you or make you anxious.)

5 *Now immediately write down, below this, how positive you now feel at this moment about life in general, again on a scale of 1–100.*

6 *Then immediately count your number of outward breaths in the next minute and write it down below this.*

7 *Now find the piece of paper you were using earlier. Is there any difference between your first and second estimates of how positive you are feeling, and your number of breaths in a minute?*

If so, why? If not, why not?

This was a simple activity to show how our bodies and minds might react to stress, and how this can affect your breathing rate. You may or may not have noticed any changes in your body, with this very simplistic test. Some people's bodies react much more or less than others in such situations. How does your breathing rate compare with the average resting rate of 12–15 breaths per minute?

Many people, when thinking about something stressful or worrying, will find that they experience physiological or bodily changes. Equally, if we become more relaxed, there will also be changes. One of the easiest ways to measure this is our breathing or heart rate. Both of these are likely to rise when we are stressed, and fall when we relax. An increase due to stress may be large or small, but even small changes will affect how our bodies are working, especially if these changes are long term or chronic. Our thinking will also be affected, and the above activity was aimed to give you a flavour of that. How positive we feel can be affected by what we've just been thinking about, or concentrating on. You may have felt more positive because you were thinking of things which have now passed, or less positive because stressful events had been brought to mind again – or you may have found there was no difference at all.

Case study – Robert

Robert is 35, and lives with his partner and their two school-age children. He has worked in a bank for ten years, and enjoys the work, but there have been rumours of redundancies over the past six months or so. He is worried about a light-headed feeling, poor concentration and tingling in his fingers and toes, which comes and goes throughout the day. He also has short episodes of feeling panic-stricken, and has already had to leave work early as he was too unwell to complete his shift. Last week, he was overcome with a feeling of panic while visiting friends, and had to make his apologies and go home. He found this very embarrassing. His doctor can find no physical problem, and suggests he might be experiencing stress, and this may be causing an increase in his breathing rate. She suggests Robert learn some form of relaxation.

The outcome of even a low level of hyperventilation is of great significance. More carbon dioxide than normal will be exhaled, producing changes in the body's delicate chemical balance. There will be a loss of carbonic acid, so the body then excretes alkalis in an effort to maintain normal acidity levels. This means that lactic acid cannot be neutralized when it builds up after exertion, causing painful muscles.

Breathing is essential for life and provides fuel for the body. So if you get that very basic of activities wrong, this can upset your whole body chemistry and produce many unusual and unexpected symptoms, which you can find yourself worrying about, making you even more tense.

Here is one breathing technique to try out now. Don't forget your relaxation exercises though. Try to find time for both. This need only take a few minutes and you may well reap huge benefits. There are always spare minutes in the day which we can use for this if time is a problem – waiting for a bus or a taxi, on the bus or train, queuing at the shops or when paying for our petrol or getting our sandwiches at lunchtime. Even the busiest of people have these spare moments – they can sometimes be the moments which make us most stressed as we are in a hurry and are made to wait, so what better use to put them to!

Try this – Scanning

1 *Breathe in while silently scanning your body for any tension.*
2 *As you breathe out, relax any tension you find.*
3 *Repeat steps 1 and 2 several times.*

Symptoms of hyperventilation

The sensations and symptoms caused by too much adrenalin, and the 'flight, fight or freeze' reaction have been explained already. Disturbing sensations such as palpitations and other cardiac symptoms may be due to the actions of adrenalin on the heart. However, most of the long-term symptoms suffered by people are due to the phenomenon of chronic over-breathing or hyperventilation, as referred to in the previous paragraphs. This hyperventilation is continuous and involuntary and usually unnoticed by the person experiencing it.

Having a better understanding of the sometimes unusual and often disturbing symptoms which over-breathing can bring about aids relaxation. So it's worth explaining these here. But if any symptom is worrying you, and causing you difficulty or distress, have it checked out by your doctor. Most of the symptoms discussed here can have other physical causes. You will probably find that your problems are not due to a physical illness, but you must just make sure. Here, in more detail, are some of these symptoms.

DIFFUSE OR LOCALIZED PAIN

Muscular aches, pains and stiffness are probably the most common symptoms. People complain of neck stiffness and soreness of aching limbs. They suffer from tension headaches and can wake in the morning with a sore neck or shoulders, sore cheek muscles from teeth clenching, or nail marks in the palms of their hands from fist clenching during the night, or day. The most characteristic pain is in the neck and shoulders.

MUSCLE SENSITIVITY

As well as muscle pain, over-breathing is associated with muscle 'sensitivity' or 'irritability'. What this means is that muscles can become unusually reactive, and this can produce, for example, tension, twitching or trembling, a tremor or a muscle spasm, often in the hands. The pain and muscular spasm can be severe.

HEADACHE

Tension headaches caused by tension and spasm in neck muscles are due to muscle irritability, and the pain can be severe and protracted. The neck muscles can be tender and painful. The headaches can last for days, and can be very disturbing and resistant to standard treatment.

FAINTNESS

Fainting is a rare complication of over-breathing. Despite this, people will often say that they feared they were going to faint in a given situation, or that they felt faint or light-headed. But there is a world of difference between feeling that one might faint and actually fainting. Only on rare occasions, where other factors such as excessive heat are operating, may a person actually faint.

DIZZINESS AND UNSTEADINESS

There may often be feelings which people describe as dizziness or vertigo, and this is very upsetting, especially the first time it happens. But the sensation is not true vertigo which makes the world seem to spin round, but is better described as unsteadiness, light-headedness, or feeling off balance. This sensation is often brought on by an imbalance in the tension in the neck muscles. One side is tighter than the other, producing a feeling of unsteadiness, or a sensation of falling to that side. It is a feeling of being unbalanced rather than dizzy.

CONCENTRATION AND MEMORY

A common outcome of over-breathing is poor concentration, and difficulty in recall. The more someone tries to remember something the more difficult it can become. Even your own phone number and address, or the names of people you know well, can suddenly become elusive information, making a person feel embarrassed and silly. This can often mean a person will become flustered, especially in public, making it difficult to remember very much about the experience. Fear of becoming flustered then makes the reality of becoming flustered more likely, due to increased anxiety and over-breathing. Problems concentrating during an event can also mean poor recall of them later on, which can be very worrying.

COUGH

For some, there may be a cough or a chronic 'tickle' in the throat, and a need to clear the throat. This may be a habit cough, or may have a physical cause, but it may also be due to a degree of tightness in the muscles of the chest or in the bronchi, the breathing tubes in the lungs.

TIGHTNESS OF THE CHEST

It can sometimes feel as if you can't get a full deep breath. This can be frightening and people sometimes throw windows open in order to get a breath, or go out into the garden or the street. They can even fill their bedrooms with fans and ionizers in the hope of warding off this symptom.

Try this – Breathing out

If you feel you just can't take a full breath, think of it this way: your lungs may simply already be full of air.

So, slow down, lower your shoulders, relax, and calmly and consciously breathe OUT. Then, in your own time, without rushing, take a normal breath in, and then continue to breathe normally and in your own time.

SIGHING AND EXCESSIVE YAWNING

Frequent sighs and yawns are also typical of over-breathing. Over-breathing can become a long-term habit of which the person may not be aware, though that person's partner or friends may well be.

PALPITATIONS

Palpitations or skipped heartbeats can also be produced. These can be particularly distressing and frightening symptoms, inevitably suggesting heart disease to the person. Palpitations can be long lasting and may even be present on examination by the doctor.

CHEST PAIN

This pain may be due to muscular contraction and irritability of the 'intercostal' muscles in the chest. Again, a frightening symptom, which of course should always be checked out by a GP to make sure it is caused by tension.

FLUSHING

People may flush or sweat, particularly in situations they find difficult or threatening. This can be on the face, neck or the upper chest. As with becoming flustered, a self-fulfilling cycle can easily establish itself. Being afraid of flushing or blushing in public can make it almost certain to happen.

DIFFICULTY SWALLOWING OR SPEAKING

These very dramatic symptoms are due to contraction of the muscles of the gullet (or oesophagus). People are aware of these contracted oesophageal muscles which they describe as a 'ball' in their gullet. They feel unable to swallow and keep trying to swallow to relieve the sensation. In doing so they make the situation worse and may experience severe discomfort or even pain.

Research, evidence and statistics

According to Dr Kenneth Hambly (2005), in an extreme case of oesophageal dysfunction, due to over-breathing, the person may not be able to swallow and may have to leave the table. Their problem is worse if they are in company or eating in a restaurant. The complaint can be demonstrated on X-ray as an oesophageal contraction.

DIGESTION

Like the other muscles in the body, the muscles which control digestion can work too fast or too slowly, producing either intestinal hurry or constipation. In any case, bowel habit is altered and cramps may also result. One part of the bowel contracts against another and severe muscular pain can result. Dr Kenneth Hambly (2005) likens this to a baby which gets cramps because of the immature neurological control of their intestine. That control is lost in adults who over-breathe, and colic or abdominal pain may result.

So, tension and over-breathing produce real symptoms, real problems, involving every area of the body. These aren't 'all in the mind', and there are rational explanations for them all. Remembering how it all works, how tension produces hormones which go everywhere in your body, preparing it for immediate action, it's not surprising that every body system is involved, every organ and every gland. But if abnormal breathing and tension are brought under control, and replaced with normal respiration and relaxation, this will all go away.

Insight

Wherever I go, I see people rushing their food. They gulp it down at lunch-time in restaurants, or on benches in the shopping areas, or they eat while they walk, or while rushing for a bus or a train. This can't be a good thing, on so many levels.

Basic relaxation prerequisites

Having learned about the symptoms brought about by tension, stress and over-breathing, and developed a better understanding, it's now time to take action and learn some basic relaxation techniques. The remainder of this chapter will teach you a method which takes about half an hour, and can be savoured and enjoyed, and also shorter methods for when you have less time, or for using on the go. Most relaxation techniques are a combination of breathing and physical skills.

Please remember that you should not practise any of these techniques if you are driving, operating machinery or if you are in charge of other people or children. And remember not to get up suddenly while following the instructions, as you may feel slightly dizzy. So, use a quiet room where you won't be disturbed, take the phone off the hook, and ignore the doorbell. Keep your eyes open to read the instructions until you can remember them, then close your eyes when you feel ready. And always allow around ten minutes for you to become fully alert again after you've practised, before you go back to your usual activities.

As already explained, none of these techniques is in any way strenuous, but if you are in any doubt about your fitness to carry them out safely, then first read the instructions, and check with your doctor if you're still unsure.

Relaxation, like any other skill, can take a bit of time to learn, so don't expect too much too soon, and don't try too hard – this will only make you more tense, not less. Simply follow the instructions in your own time, and allow the relaxation to happen on its own. You may even find, to begin with, that you can only relax fleetingly before tension returns, or your mind begins to wander. Don't be concerned about this, simply return to what you were doing and continue.

With practice, you will find that you relax more and more deeply and efficiently. In time you should also be able to practise these techniques without the instructions to help you, so that you can use them anywhere and anytime that you need them. Some people find these techniques work fully straight away. For others it can take a few practices, and then it begins to fall into place.

Insight

I find if I place my hands on each side of my face, from chin to forehead, over gently closed eyes, allowing space for my nose to breathe, and then apply very gentle pressure, this is very relaxing and feels very secure.

Progressive muscle relaxation

Let's begin with 'Total Relaxation'. This long and slow method is based on 'progressive muscle relaxation', which was discussed earlier in the book. You should allow around 30 minutes for this, and try to practise two or three times a week. Try this out when you're already feeling quite relaxed until you get the hang of it. Choose a time when you're not too tired, or you may fall asleep. That won't do any harm, it's just more effective if you are awake throughout.

Try this – Total Relaxation

First, have a read through the instructions; don't do anything yet. What you will be doing is not at all strenuous, but does involve tensing your muscles. If you are in any doubt about your physical fitness to try this, check with your doctor. If you have raised blood pressure, it is probably better not to try this activity (any of the others in the book, which don't involve tensing muscles, will be suitable).

Try out this technique with your eyes open at first, so that you can read what to do. However, it is much more relaxing if you can work your way through it without having to look at the instructions. After a practice or two, it should be fairly easy to remember the method, and it can then be done with your eyes closed.

1 *Lie on your back, or sit up in a comfortable chair, preferably with some support for your head and arms. Carry out the following very, very slowly...*
2 *Breathe slowly and evenly for a few moments, allowing yourself to unwind a little bit with each outward breath. Feel yourself slowing down, bit by bit.*
3 *Now clench your fists and hold them really tight for five or six seconds. Feel the tension. Now release them suddenly. Let all the tension go, and relax them completely. You may notice a feeling of warmth and heaviness in your fingers, hands and lower arms. This is an important sign that you are relaxing properly.*
4 *Now hunch up your shoulders. Feel that tension. Hold it for five or six seconds. Now let your shoulders slump suddenly. Let them relax. Feel the relief. Let your breathing slow even further. Now push your head back a little into its support, tensing your neck and head slightly. Feel the tension. Now let your head return to its position, and r...e...l...a...x....*

(Contd)

5 Next, frown and close your eyes tightly, purse your lips, clench your jaw and press your tongue against the roof of your mouth. Feel all sorts of tension in your head and face. Hold it. Now suddenly let it all go. Let all the tension go. Let your jaw sag and your mouth open slightly. Breathe slowly and evenly. Enjoy the feelings of relaxation you are creating for yourself.

6 Now arch your back slightly. Hold it for a second or two. Now relax. Enjoy that relaxation.

7 Pull in your stomach hard, harder. Hold it for a few seconds. Now let it go. Breathe slowly and evenly. Enjoy the feelings of relaxation for a moment.

8 Point your toes away from you, and curl your toes under, tightly. Feel the tension throughout your legs. Hold it for a few seconds... now suddenly let go and relax again. Let even more tension go as you breathe out.

9 Your whole body will now feel heavy and completely relaxed. Your breathing will be slow and gentle. Allow yourself to feel heavier and heavier, and more and more relaxed. Enjoy these feelings for a few moments or longer if you have the time.

10 When you feel ready, finish your session gradually. In your own time, with no rush, allow yourself to become more alert. Have a yawn and a stretch if you feel like it. Allow at least ten minutes to rouse yourself completely, until you are fully alert again.

After a few weeks, if you are relaxing well with Total Relaxation, you can move on to the following techniques for relaxing more quickly. You should try out these methods, and choose those that suit you best for when you need to relax quickly. Unlike Total Relaxation, these can be used anywhere, anytime. There may be several which suit you for different situations. You can still use Total Relaxation anytime you feel like a nice long relaxation session.

Autogenic training

This is very similar to progressive muscle relaxation, but doesn't involve any tensing of muscles. Johannes Schultz first described it in 1932. The aim is to influence the autonomic nervous system by focusing on a part of the body, and repeating the idea either verbally or as a thought, that this part of the body is changing in some way, most typically becoming warmer or heavier. 'Autogenic' means produced or created by oneself, and the idea is to induce a feeling of warmth and heaviness throughout the whole body, by working gradually through the arms, legs, stomach, head, and so on. The technique, Quick Relax 1, which you'll have a chance to try shortly, is a version of this technique. Autogenic techniques can also be used in the same way to encourage calm breathing, or a calm and steady heartbeat.

Insight

Most people aim to get to where they're going just in time for appointments, the cinema, the train, the school run, theatre, or whatever. Try aiming to be ten minutes early, and you'll find you're far less hurried, and there will even be time for that busy traffic, broken nail, or unexpected phone call.

QUICKER WAYS TO RELAX THE BODY

Here are some techniques which are suited to relaxing the body, some taking seconds, some a few minutes. Try them all, allowing between five and ten minutes for each, and find which suits you best. Think about where you could use them too, as they can all be done when you are out and about. Most can be done lying down, but they can all be done standing or sitting too. Work on your favourites several times a week, to become proficient, and then use these whenever and wherever you want.

Try these – Quick relaxation exercises

Quick Relax 1
Lie or sit comfortably, and allow your breathing to become slow and even. Now concentrate on your hands and arms. Don't tense them. Just concentrate on allowing all the tension to drain away from them. Allow them to feel heavier and a little warmer. Heavier and a little warmer.

(Contd)

Continue concentrating like this on each part of your body in turn, in the same order as for Total Relaxation – hands and arms, shoulders, neck and head, face, back and stomach, legs and feet – letting all the tension drain away, and allowing them to feel heavier and warmer, without tensing them first. Enjoy the feeling of relaxation you have produced for a few moments or more if you have time, then finish your session as for Total Relaxation.

Quick Relax 2

Follow the instructions as for Total Relaxation, but speed up the whole process, so that you can become relaxed within a minute or two. Finish off as before.

Quick Relax 3

Lie or sit comfortably, allowing your breathing to become slow and regular.

Now, all at the same time, deliberately tense up tightly your whole body, and hold it for a few seconds – hands, arms, shoulders, neck and head, face, back and stomach, legs and feet. Then suddenly, let it all go, and allow relaxation to take over.

Repeat the whole process once more if necessary.

Enjoy the relaxation for a few moments or longer if you have time, then finish off your session as before.

Quick Relax 4

This quick exercise helps loosen the muscles in your neck and upper back.

Stand or sit, stretch your arms out from your sides and shake your hands vigorously for about ten seconds. Combine this with two or three deep breaths.

Countdown 1

Sit, stand or lie down.

Slow down and focus on your breathing.

Now count silently backwards from ten to zero, saying the next number silently each time you breathe out.

String Puppet
Sit or stand.

Let your breath go, then take in a deep breath, hold it for a second or two, then let it go with a sigh of relief, dropping your shoulders and slumping your whole body like a puppet whose strings have been cut.

Repeat this once.

Countdown 2
Sit, stand or lie down quietly.

Now do a very slow and silent countdown from ten to zero, imagining yourself unwinding and letting go a little bit more with each downward count.

Repeat if necessary.

A good night's sleep

Even the most effective relaxation technique, practised diligently, will have its benefits hampered without adequate restful sleep each night. Having difficulty getting to sleep or staying asleep, or wakening early are all very common difficulties, meaning that sleep deprivation is remarkably common, especially with the twenty-first century lifestyle. Lack of enough refreshing sleep brings about all kinds of difficulties such as:

▶ *fatigue (especially dangerous if driving)*
▶ *tension*

- *irritability*
- *poor concentration*
- *poor memory*
- *feeling under par*
- *stumbling over words*
- *difficulty making decisions*
- *increased likelihood of making mistakes, especially simple ones such as with numbers, times or dates.*

Some people may need as much as ten hours' sleep a night while others need much less. The average person needs between seven and eight hours a night. If you find yourself sleepy during the day, you probably need more sleep at night. Or, if you sleep longer on the weekends than during the week, you probably need more sleep during the week.

Insight

Have you noticed how infectious a yawn can be? Even just talking about it can set me off. So just talking about getting off to bed, nodding off, or getting 'some winks', can begin the process of unwinding, ready for sleep.

TIPS FOR A GOOD REST

Here are some ideas for getting a good night's sleep, but if problems persist, the doctor can usually offer further help.

Keep cool
Too many heavy covers can make your body temperature too high for deep sleep.

Draw the curtains or blinds
The absence of light is crucial to sleep, as this allows the release of melatonin, a hormone produced in the pineal gland when we sleep. If your bedroom is light, perhaps due to the time of year, or street lights, draw the curtains or pull the blinds. Blackout blinds are useful, especially for shift workers who have to sleep during the day.

Reduce noise
Quiet is also essential for most people, though some prefer low-key sound. Consider using earplugs if there is noise from the street or from neighbours, or if you have to sleep during the day.

Big bed size
The bed should offer comfortable support, and enough space for free and easy movement. If you are part of a couple, consider a queen or king bed, as space is relaxing.

Baths and showers
If you like a bath before bedtime, make it two hours before bedtime, because it will increase your temperature, and as your temperature comes down, this can encourage sleep. A shower just before bedtime will just wake you up, and is best kept for the morning.

Bed is for sleeping
You want your body to associate the bed with sleeping and making love, and nothing else. If you like to read or watch TV before going to sleep, or at other times of the day, make sure to do this on a chair or sofa, preferably one in the living room. If you have to read or watch TV on the bed, make sure you are sitting up with covers and perhaps cushions on the bed. Only turn down the covers and lie down when you are going to sleep.

Relaxation
Wind down for at least half an hour before going to bed. The mind, thinking and brainwaves have to be ready for sleep. Once in bed, any method of relaxation or breathing technique which works for you will help ease this process gently along. This will help getting to sleep as well as getting back to sleep if you wake during the night or early in the morning.

Keep to your schedule, even on weekends
Going to sleep and getting up at about the same time every day gives your body the cues it needs to nod off. Catching up on sleep over the weekend will usually result in a sleepless Sunday night.

Exercise regularly – but not too close to bedtime

Exercising during the day increases the time your body spends in deep sleep. But exercising less than three hours before going to sleep can leave you too stimulated for sleep.

Reduce caffeine, cigarettes and alcohol

Avoid caffeine in coffee, drinks and food at least six hours before bedtime. Cigarettes are a powerful stimulant that can keep you awake for hours. And though you may feel like nodding off after you have a drink or two, once the effects of alcohol wear off, sleep can actually become more disturbed.

Early dinner

Eating a big meal in the evening doesn't encourage sleep. It is better to have a light dinner no later than 6:30 p.m. But no need to go to bed hungry. If you need a snack, opt for something like wholemeal bread/toast, an oaty cereal or a milky drink – all are known to increase levels of the brain chemical serotonin, which is thought to produce deeper sleep.

Still can't sleep?

If you still can't sleep, and have been wide awake for half an hour, it's best to get up and do something rather than lying in bed. What you do when up must be low key and non-stimulating, even boring. Perhaps the ironing, read something restful, or maybe watch some quiet TV, until you feel sleepy again. Then go back to bed.

Abdominal breathing

Another faster way to relax, which can be particularly helpful when trying to sleep, is abdominal breathing. This is also known as diaphragmatic, or 'sleep-style' breathing. Watch a sleeping cat or dog and you'll see its tummy rising and falling slowly, while its chest remains still. That's what you're aiming for.

Try this – Abdominal breathing

1 *Lie or sit comfortably, with good support.*
2 *Put one hand flat on your navel, the other on your upper chest. No pressure, just resting there gently.*

3 *Let your breath out, then breathe in very gently – allowing your tummy to rise under your hand as you do so.*

4 *In your own time, breathe out again gently, and notice your tummy fall again.*

5 *Continue this gentle breathing, trying to have as little movement of the other hand on your upper chest as you can.*

6 *With practice you will manage to breathe in this way without using your hands to guide you, and also when you are standing up.*

Aids to relaxation

In the past few decades, more and more gadgets and gizmos have been invented to encourage relaxation and reduce stress.

Stress dots and stress cards work through contact with the skin, and are based on measuring skin temperature, which tends to be lower when you are stressed or tense. When you are stressed there is an increase in muscle tension, the blood vessels near the skin's surface constrict and the temperature of your hands and feet decreases. Similarly, as you relax, your hands and feet become warmer and blood flows more freely. The colour change of the stress dot or stress card simply and graphically demonstrates the changes in the body's stress levels. You place the dot on the fleshy part of the joint between the first finger and thumb on the back of the hand. The inside of the wrist can also provide an effective reading.

Tactile toys take things beyond simply measuring how tense you are. They give the hands something to do, for example, stretching, bending or squeezing, and this can have a relaxing effect for many people. The rhythmic movement of some 'executive toys' has a similar relaxing effect – Newton's cradle for example (six metal balls swinging in a rhythmic pattern), or the movement of a 'slinky' (long coiled spring). All of these effects can now be reproduced on a computer, and there are now numerous software packages available. Much more on all of this in Chapter 10.

All of these can be really useful, but there are drawbacks. Cost is probably the main drawback, as most gadgets are quite expensive, with some priced into the thousands of pounds. However, some cost only a few pennies, or pounds. Stress dots, squeezers and juggling balls are examples of the lower price range. Also, unless you are going for the more expensive items such as computer software, they are of limited effectiveness. Stress dots, for example, are reacting to temperature, which can vary for many reasons other than stress levels. The other main drawback is that you can't use most of them at work or out and about – imagine juggling during a business meeting, or at an interview!

However, they are fun and something a little different. Every way of relaxing has its time and place.

Some of these gadgets also aim to relax the mind as well as the body. So, it is to relaxing the mind and thinking processes that we now turn to in the next chapter.

Research, evidence and statistics

Music appears to enhance progressive (total) relaxation, and this combination may be more effective than either of these treatments alone.

V. Kibler and M. Rider (1983) *Journal of Clinical Psychology.*

KEY POINTS

Look back over this chapter and choose the TWO pieces of information you found to be most interesting or helpful. Write these here, or go back and underline or highlight them in some way.

1 ....

2 ....

Look back over this chapter and choose the FOUR practical suggestions you found to be most useful. Write these here, or go back and underline or highlight them in some way.

1 ....

2 ....

3 ....

4 ....

Which TWO techniques or suggestions from this chapter would you like to try out straight away?

Write these here, or go back and underline or highlight them in some way.

1 ....

2 ....

Which TWO techniques or suggestions from this chapter would you like to work towards using regularly?

(Contd)

Write these here, or go back and underline or highlight them in some way.

1 ....

2 ....

6

Relaxed body language

In this chapter you will learn:
- *to avoid give-away signs of tension*
- *how to relax on the move*
- *ways to look and sound relaxed*
- *that just looking relaxed can help you to feel relaxed.*

Body language

You've learned a great deal now about tension, and physical relaxation techniques. You know what tension is, and how it feels. And you know what it looks like too. This means that when you aren't relaxed, this will automatically show in your body, and in your body language, or 'non-verbal communication'. We can usually tell just by looking at someone if they are tense.

Body language partly explains how good actors can become such different people so easily. First they get the posture and body language just right. So actors like David Jason are equally believable as Del Boy in *Only Fools and Horses* and DI Frost in *A Touch of Frost*. Michael Crawford completely transformed himself from a whimpering 'Frank Spencer' into the powerful depiction of the Phantom of the Opera. Actors like Patricia Routledge, Tom Courtney and Robert de Niro seem to be able to transform themselves simply by use of posture and voice, so that we are sometimes surprised when we see the 'real' them for the first time in a chat show, for example.

How you're feeling translates into your body language, tone of voice and conversation, largely without your being aware of this. But the people we interact with do notice it, without realizing it, and receive messages through our body language. And these messages will override what we are actually saying. It's not what we say, it's how we say it.

Try this – Mirror image

You'll need a full-length mirror for this, and an empty room, preferably with no one else around. (If you have a video camera you could use that instead of a mirror.) You'll also need some paper and a pen or pencil.

1   *Stand in front of a full-length mirror, as you would normally stand. Look at yourself closely. Take a few moments. Now move away and walk past the mirror. How were you standing? How did you walk past? Try to take a step outside of yourself for a moment to think. Be a fly on the wall. Imagine you are in a TV programme. What impression are you giving? Be honest. Jot down your thoughts on your notepaper.*

2   *How do you come into a room? Take a moment or two before you do this, to try to imagine this really clearly, and feel the way you would be feeling if there were five or six people in it, and you didn't know any of them.*

Go out of the room now, close the door, then come back into the room, the way you would. Position your full-length mirror to check this out if you can.

Now describe what happened under these headings:

▶ *Body posture (upright, stooped etc.)*
▶ *Speed*
▶ *Did you knock?*
▶ *Did your head come in first, then your body? Did you come half way in then hold back a little? Or did you come in some other way?*
▶ *How far did you open the door?*

> ▶ How did you hold your head?
> ▶ Where were your arms and what were they doing (e.g. by your sides, in pockets, holding on to something for comfort)?
> ▶ Shoulders (hunched up, tense)?
> ▶ What about eye contact when you came into the room. Where were you looking?
> ▶ How/where would you sit or stand (first possible seat, corner, near the door, as quickly as you can, etc.)?
>
> 3 Now think about relaxed and confident people – how do they come into a room, in the same situation (describe under same headings)?
>
> ▶ Body posture
> ▶ Speed
> ▶ Head come in first, then body? Or another way?
> ▶ How far would they open the door for themselves?
> ▶ How would they hold their head?
> ▶ Arms and hands?
> ▶ Shoulders?
> ▶ Eye contact? Where would they look?
> ▶ Where/how would they sit?

So, there is a lot about body language when coming into a room that lets people know how tense you are. It's not just about muscle tension. It's also about posture, how you carry yourself, and what you do with your hands, and so on. Body language most certainly matters. In self-defence classes, those attending are told that when they are out in the street they shouldn't walk or stand like a victim. They should walk upright, relaxed, and with confidence. Muggers always go for the person who already looks like a victim.

It is possible to be like an actor, and practise having the body language of a relaxed person. This can be practised at home when no one's about, to get a feel for it. With a bit of practice it will come more naturally, without thinking about it. The best of it is that if you stand and walk without tension, you will actually feel and be more relaxed. 'Partial Relaxation' helps you to practise this too.

Relaxation on the go

So far we have taught you how to relax the whole body. But what if you are using all or part of your body to do something, like walking, driving or working at a computer? How do you keep the rest of your body relaxed while you are using part of it? What if relaxing your whole body would cause a problem with something you're doing? Other examples would include using the telephone, working at a check-out, taking part in a meeting, hoovering, using a computer or laptop, giving a presentation, doing the weekly shop, talking to people – in fact all sorts of common everyday activities.

People often find that they are very tense when carrying out everyday tasks, and can find themselves gripping the phone too tightly, holding facial muscles taut when talking to people, or experiencing neck or back pain from tension when using a computer or supermarket check-out till. The answer to this is to learn 'Partial Relaxation'.

This helps you to be able to use parts of your body, for example, your hands for writing while you are talking to people, and yet keep the remainder of your body as relaxed as possible. Not completely relaxed, but with just enough tension for the job in hand, and no more. It's that extra bit of unnecessary tension that is the problem.

Use Total Relaxation, or any other method which works for you, immediately before trying this new technique. As before, you may have to refer to these instructions for the first few times, and then you should manage without these.

Try this – Partial Relaxation

Make sure that you are already completely relaxed before you try this type of relaxation. The idea is to be able to learn to relax the remainder of your body as much as possible, while using part of it. You should allow ten to 15 minutes. Here is what to do:

1 *Lie or sit, totally relaxed for a few moments, eyes lightly closed.*

2 *Now raise your hands, and begin moving them in the air as if writing, typing or some other relevant action. Try to keep the rest of your body completely relaxed as you do this. Scan the rest of your body for any unnecessary tension, and release it. Continue doing this for a few moments.*

3 *Now, gently open your eyes, and slowly look around the room, keeping your head still. Move your eyes only, and again, try to keep the rest of your body relaxed and at ease.*

4 *Now look around again by moving your head a little, again, keeping the rest of your body relaxed.*

5 *Next, keeping your head and eyes still, try saying a few words, again keeping your body relaxed. Any words will do. Scan your body for unnecessary tension and release it. Now relax completely again for a few moments.*

6 *Next, sit up slowly, and practise sitting up, eyes open, totally relaxed for a few moments. Release any unnecessary tension. Keep your whole body relaxed and at ease.*

7 *Now very slowly stand up and see if you can stand in a relaxed way, with no more tension than required. Release any unnecessary tension. After standing still for a few moments, walk around a little, pick something up and carry it, then replace it – all the time checking for and releasing any unnecessary tension. Use only the minimum of tension needed in the muscles which you are using.*

8 *Now gradually lie or sit back down, and relax your whole body once again. Close your eyes gently, and allow all tension to drain away from your whole body. Enjoy the feeling of complete relaxation for a few moments or more if you have time.*

9 *When you feel ready, finish your session gradually. In your own time with no rush, allow yourself to become more alert. Have a yawn and a stretch if you feel like it. Allow yourself between five and ten minutes to become fully alert again.*

The remainder of this chapter on body language will give you some more ideas on how to behave in a more relaxed way. Read through and see if some of these will be useful for you. Highlight anything you find particularly useful.

Insight

Have you noticed how you have certain clothes that you just feel really comfortable in? And then there are others which irritate and annoy you, and always need checking or adjusting? Aim to have more of the comfortable ones, and far fewer of the others.

Making things better

Much of the body language which shows tension arises from a need for comfort and security. We are nervous and ill at ease, and unsure of ourselves, and just like children, seek comfort from contact with another person or object – just like a child runs to their mother, or clings to their security blanket or doll. As adults, this need has reduced to clinging to a handbag, or a newspaper or a pen, or making sure we have someone beside us at social events. Tension can make us hunch up our shoulders, nearer and nearer to our ears. People can even ask you if you are feeling cold because of this. So let them drop.

Stooped posture and poor eye contact also arise from a wish to make ourselves as small and unnoticeable as we can. Of course, all of this does the opposite, and simply draws attention to us. Just like the tall person who is embarrassed by their height, and walks with a stoop so that we won't notice it. We notice it all the more.

POSTURE

An open and relaxed posture is usually best at all times, preferably with little or nothing in your hands. Open posture means comfortably upright, shoulders comfortably back, head up, with no barriers formed by your hands or arms. Arms comfortably by your side, or open hands resting easily on your lap when sitting convey quiet relaxed confidence. The relaxation and breathing exercises covered already will make this posture easier to achieve.

Avoid walking or standing with palm in palm behind your back (like the Duke of Edinburgh, or a policeman) as this is a sign of authority or dominance. Likewise, keep your hands out of your pockets, especially if you tend to jingle your change!

Unwanted tension can make you form a fist with your hands, or cling to a handbag, briefcase or drink, like a comfort blanket. This will be noticed unconsciously, or even consciously by those you are with. Avoid folding your arms as this creates a barrier, and can be interpreted as a lack of interest, or even disagreement or disapproval. This will inhibit other people from talking to you. When standing, avoid leaning on furniture or the doorway. Again, this can be done for comfort, but can come over as somewhat odd or even intimidating or dominating.

> *Sometimes I just sits and thinks, and sometimes I just sits.*
>
> Satchel Paige, US baseball player, 1906–82

When sitting, sit up well. This is good for your back too! Slouching into a chair or a corner can be comforting, but looks defensive and uninviting. So sit up and lean forward a little towards others you might be talking to. This shows interest and encourages people. Crossed legs or ankles also tend to make you appear tense, defensive or negative.

HANDSHAKES

A handshake can give an unfavourable impression of us which is hard to shift.

Sometimes we can be concentrating so much on ourselves and the impression we are making, that we forget to really shake the other person's hand at all! That is, we can give what is known as the 'dead-fish' or 'cold-fish' handshake which is what it sounds like, a cold and limp handshake that does not engage with the other person's hand at all. This is a universally unpopular handshake, and most people relate it to the person giving it having a weak character or being rather nervous. Those giving this handshake are often totally unaware that they are doing it.

The other common sign of tension or anxiety is the sweaty palm, and this can produce another disliked handshake, a damp one. This gives the game away completely. It also gives a very unfavourable first impression. To avoid this, make sure that your hands are unclenched and out of your pockets, and hold them open well in advance of meeting someone, as this helps to allow the sweat to evaporate naturally. Alternatively dry them, unseen, on a handkerchief, napkin (or, if worst comes to worst, on your clothing), before shaking hands – it makes all the difference. It's all about recognizing the pitfalls and being prepared for them.

The best form of handshake is single-handed, dry and fairly firm, with both your hand and that of the person you are meeting in a vertical position. This, teamed with good eye contact and a warm smile, is an assertive and relaxed form of greeting. Avoid giving a palm down handshake as this indicates dominance, or palm upward as this suggests that you are passive or submissive.

Insight

A person's handshake leaves a very strong impression, and it's also part of that 'first impression' which tends to stick. So it's something simple, which you can easily change for the better.

EYE CONTACT

If we are unsure of ourselves, we can find it difficult to make eye contact with other people. It can be easier to look at the floor, or out of the window when talking to someone, only making eye contact occasionally, if at all. But this makes the other person feel uncomfortable, and that you are not really interested in them. So what to do?

Making eye contact for about two-thirds of the time is usually about right for a comfortable conversation, but judge this for yourself. Women tend to use eye contact a little more than men do. Avoid staring constantly – this doesn't show deep interest as is sometimes thought, but is more likely to appear a little aggressive, and is very off-putting. Similarly, if you look away too much, this can make you seem uninterested, tense or distracted. So on a first meeting with someone, as a very rough guide, look for three–four seconds, then glance away for one–two seconds, then look back for another three–four seconds and so on. It's probably better to look more when you're listening, and look away more when you're talking. It's also better to break eye contact in a downward direction, as this shows interest. Breaking eye contact in an upward or sideways direction, or keeping eye contact for too long, can seem disconcerting or negative.

If you are standing and there is a height difference, it's always better to try to sit down somewhere, so that your eye level becomes closer to the other person's. If you are a woman who would prefer to be taller, don't make the mistake of wearing very high heels to compensate, as this only distorts your posture and walking. A small to medium heel is best. Confident people are always perceived as being taller than they are, so just walk tall!

TONE OF VOICE

Almost as important as your body language is your voice and how you use it. Body language and tone of voice together convey most of what we communicate to others. We have all seen and heard people engaged in conversation at a bit of a distance in the street or at the other side of a room, and even without hearing the actual words they are using, we can make a pretty good stab at working out what is going on – an argument, a discussion, romance, everyday conversation, and so on.

Many of us have been taken to task over something we thought we had said quite innocently by the criticism, 'It's not what you said, it's the way that you said it.' So tone of voice is important, and aiming for a warm, gentle, low-pitched and friendly tone, in tune with what is being said to you, is well worthwhile.

Strangely enough, it is often a person's warm and welcoming tone of voice which makes others perceive them as friendly or a 'good listener'. If you're not sure how you sound, try recording it and have a listen.

Insight

It's well documented that Margaret Thatcher, UK prime minister from 1979 to 1990, took lessons to lower her rather high-pitched speaking voice, to improve the impression she was giving.

Try this – Listen to yourself

Here is an activity for making your tone of voice more interesting and more relaxed and confident. You can practise this whenever you want if you find it helpful. You can record this to see how you do, but you don't need to do so if you don't want to.

Listening to the sound of your own voice can be useful for building confidence. You may be unused to being allowed to speak freely, so find it threatening when you have to speak for yourself. If you're not happy with what you hear, do more practising like this and it will improve things.

Here's what to do.

1 *If you have young children around, choose one of their books, sit one or more of them down, and read a story aloud to them. If not, just find a book of children's stories, or a newspaper or magazine story, and read it out loud on your own. Read it to your pet if you have one. Sounds silly, but it's worth it!*

2 *When you are reading, try to add as much interest to it as you can using your voice alone. Think about how actors read stories to children on TV, and let your voice reflect what's happening in the story – the emotions, the danger, the action. Change the pace, the volume, the pitch, the tone. Do voices*

HEAD POSITION

When talking to people, having your head tilted downwards
slightly can appear disapproving, or dismissive. Tilted further
down appears passive and withdrawn and is very off-putting to
others. Aim to have your head upright and straight on to someone
you're talking to, or better still slightly tilted to one side, as this
shows interest and support for what's being said. Nodding at
appropriate moments, and using facial expressions which reflect
interest and understanding are all good for building rapport with
someone.

BODY POSITIONS

If standing having a conversation with one other person,
don't stand straight on to them, as this can seem intrusive and
dominating. Standing at about a 90-degree angle to the other
person is about right. Three people will usually stand in an equal-
sided triangle, and so on. Most of us do this quite naturally
without thinking. Have a look at people standing talking in the
street or in a shop or pub, and you'll see this in action.

TOUCHING

It's also best to avoid touching people while talking to them,
unless they are very close friends or family. We probably all know
someone who goes around annoying everyone without realizing
it because they are habitual 'touchers' – on the arm, on the hand,
sometimes back slapping. Nervousness and tension can also
encourage this behaviour. Best to be avoided.

GESTURES

Too many hand or arm gestures are distracting. It's also best to avoid pointing at someone while you speak, as this appears aggressive to the other person. A few well placed but simple gestures add interest and show enthusiasm. Try to notice what you are doing with your hands and arms when talking to people. Here again, nervousness or tension can produce many distracting gestures, as you seek comfort from your body, your clothing or other objects. So you might keep touching your hair, or a more current habit, running your hands through it. You might fiddle with objects – usually pens, earrings or necklaces. Ask a friend if you're not sure. Just becoming aware of the possibility will help you to notice it for yourself.

PERSONAL SPACE

We all have an invisible barrier around us called our personal space. This is the space we only let people we know very well come into. Family, friends or loved ones can come into this space without us becoming uncomfortable. This space varies from person to person and sometimes depends on where and how we were brought up, but it is usually somewhere between half a metre and a metre, although it can be much more, or considerably less. So it is important that you don't invade the other person's space, and make sure they are comfortable with where you are sitting or standing. So keep a comfortable distance away from someone you are talking to.

Our own physical body possesses a wisdom which we who inhabit it lack.

Henry Miller, US author, 1891–1980

Sometimes it's easier for you to sit down first, and ask the other person to choose where they want to sit, or whether they would rather stand. You may both be standing anyway, which allows the person to maintain a comfortable distance. So if the person moves away from you as you are talking, don't move back in closer, or you may be making them uncomfortable. They may just move away again, and if you follow again, you may end up chasing them round the room! Seriously though, this can and does happen – look around the next time you are at a party or other social event where people are standing talking. Is anyone chasing anyone else slowly round the room?

If someone we don't know well enters our personal space we can become extremely uncomfortable; the closer to us they come, the worse we feel. There are exceptions to this though, such as when we're on a crowded bus or train, or in a packed waiting room. But as soon as the crowd subsides, we feel uncomfortable being so close to others, and people will soon tend to spread out again.

Summary of relaxed body language

BODY

- ▶ *comfortably upright posture*
- ▶ *head comfortably up*
- ▶ *shoulders relaxed, down and back*
- ▶ *regular (about 2/3 of time) and direct eye contact*
- ▶ *no unnecessary tension*
- ▶ *little or nothing in hands*
- ▶ *no barriers with hands or arms*
- ▶ *give people their space.*

First impressions do matter. So, give a good one. Walk the walk and talk the talk.

VOICE

- ▶ *slow*
- ▶ *steady*
- ▶ *low-pitched*
- ▶ *warm.*

HANDSHAKES

- ▶ *relaxed but firm*
- ▶ *not limp*

- *upright/vertical*
- *not damp!*

ENTERING A ROOM
- *think before you go in, and get your posture and appearance right*
- *open the door firmly*
- *enter with confidence*
- *enter like you mean it*
- *make eye contact immediately with those in the room*
- *don't rush to a corner – move confidently to join someone central.*

HABITS TO AVOID
- *jingling change in pocket*
- *hands in pockets*
- *fiddling with anything (pen, jewellery, clothing)*
- *clutching for comfort (handbag, pen, notes etc.)*
- *slouching*
- *touching people*
- *too many gestures*
- *running hands through hair.*

CLOTHING AND APPEARANCE
- *loose and comfortable*
- *layers best for all temperature conditions*
- *suited to the situation – nothing too eye-catching*
- *smart and clean*
- *hair neat, presentable and unsurprising.*

Insight

There is such a lot more you can learn about body language simply by looking at other people. Just calmly observe others when you can – on a train or a bus, in a queue, walking around the shops – without seeming rude, of course. Try to spot relaxed people, and tense people, walking, talking, in meetings, wherever. What is it about their body language that you are reading?

Cultural differences

It is worth remembering that all that has been said so far about body language is most likely to apply to two people from the same cultural background and in a Western-type society. When people from the same cultural or ethnic background interact with one another, they can very easily read the other's body language, as they share that language. But each cultural background has its own specific body language, especially with respect to gestures, personal space and comforting; even a nod of the head can have a different meaning. So, if you and the other person are from the same background, your own particular set of rules will apply. If you are talking to someone from a cultural group different from your own, be aware of these differences and check this out with the person if you are at all unsure of anything.

Finally, don't try to do too much all at once. If you try to apply all of these ideas about body language you may come into a room looking strange, and maybe slightly distracted. It's best to concentrate on one thing at a time, maybe your general posture, and work on that for a while, before moving on to what you're doing with your hands, your head or your eyes. Body language is the habit of a lifetime. It takes a little time and effort to make changes. But the positive side of this is that with each change, the next one comes a little more easily. The positive feedback in how other people react to these changes is also likely to encourage you.

KEY POINTS

Look back over this chapter and choose the THREE pieces of information you found to be most interesting or helpful. Write these here, or go back and underline or highlight them in some way.

1 ....

2 ....

3 ....

Look back over this chapter and choose the FOUR practical suggestions you found to be most useful. Write these here, or go back and underline or highlight them in some way.

1 ....

2 ....

3 ....

4 ....

Which TWO techniques or suggestions from this chapter would you like to try out straight away? Write these here, or go back and underline or highlight them in some way.

1 ....

2 ....

Which technique or suggestion from this chapter would you like to work towards using regularly?

Write this here, or go back and underline or highlight it in some way.

....

7

A relaxed mind and
calm thinking

In this chapter you will learn:
- *lots of ways to calm your mind*
- *how to use imagery and visualization to help you*
- *to spot how your thinking is making you tense*
- *how some sounds can be calming.*

So far we've been focusing almost exclusively on relaxing the
body. But sometimes it's relaxing the mind which is the main
problem. Even with a relaxed body, it is possible for the mind
still to be churning away. Being able to relax physically will
go some way to helping the mind to relax. Getting plenty of
restful sleep is also a prerequisite for a relaxed mind, and this has
been covered in Chapter 5. But sometimes a bit more help
is needed.

The key point in relaxing the mind is to be aware that simply
telling yourself not to think about something or trying to take
your mind off your worries won't achieve a thing. The more you
try to do this, sometimes the worse it gets. Why? Because the
more you do this the more you are actually paying attention to,
and concentrating on the thoughts you are trying to eliminate.
Sometimes these thoughts can even assume even greater
proportions and seem much larger than they really are, simply
because you keep concentrating on them so much.

No, the key tip here is that the way to get your mind off your worries is to give it something else to think about. And the way to make it relax, is to give it something relaxing to think about.

How to relax the mind

Imagination is the highest kite one can fly.

Lauren Bacall, actress, born 1924

What you think about is very much down to individual preferences. The main thing is that you imagine it as clearly and in as much detail as possible, and that you bring in as many of your senses as you can. See clearly in your mind's eye, smell the smells, hear the sounds, feel what you can touch with your fingers, or feel on your face, and so on.

Lots of suggestions are given here, and what to do is try them out and see what works best for you. Everyone is different and you will find some work better than others. Techniques from this chapter will often work well together, or combined with methods for relaxing the body. Music and imagery often make a good combination, and would be one idea. Or the sound of waves lapping gently on the sand can markedly enhance the effects of Total Relaxation for many people.

Like physical relaxation techniques, everything in this chapter is a new skill, and some techniques need a bit of practice before you get the best from them. But the rewards make it worth the effort.

Try these – Mental relaxation exercises

First use whatever method you have found works best for you to relax your body – either Total or Quick Relaxation, or perhaps 1-2-3 breathing from Chapter 3.

Now try out the following methods, and see what works best for you. For each one, close your eyes, and try concentrating on it in your mind's eye, for at least one minute.

Focus 1
Repeat silently and very slowly in your mind, a word or phrase such as:

▶ *r...e...l...a...x*
▶ *p...e...a...c...e*
▶ *calm... and... quiet*
▶ *slow... down*
▶ *calmness... is... easing... my... mind.*

Note here which works best for you.

Focus 2
Focus your mind absolutely on one of these:

▶ *a much-loved face*
▶ *a favourite place*
▶ *a well-loved picture.*

Note here which works best for you.

Focus 3 (introduced in Chapter 3)

Picture in your mind as clearly and in as much detail as you can, a calming scene such as:

▶ *waves lapping on the seashore*
▶ *branches blowing gently in the breeze*
▶ *boats bobbing in the harbour*
▶ *corn swaying in the breeze*
▶ *deep dark green velvet.*

Note here which works best for you.

Creative people often find it much easier to imagine scenes or pictures. Words and phrases can be easy for most people. Remember, practice is often needed to become good at this, but it can be especially effective in relaxing the mind. With practice, these techniques can be a trigger for complete mind and body relaxation.

Insight

The mind has immense power. Think one positive thought and you'll probably feel a little brighter, think two or three and it's pretty much guaranteed.

Relaxed thinking

This topic was touched on earlier in the book, but there is much more to learn. We all know people who remain positive and unbowed in the face of difficult circumstances, and others who simply cave in and give up hope. Then there are people who remain cheerful and determined no matter what life throws at them – and others who can always find something to grumble about. It's the old idea of whether we see the glass as half full or half empty. The difference lies purely in how these individuals think about their situation. The difference is in their attitude to life – how they think about it.

> *The greatest discovery of any generation is that human beings can alter their lives by altering the attitudes of their minds.*
>
> Albert Schweitzer, French theologian, musician, philosopher and physician

How we think and how we see a situation has a powerful influence on how we deal with life's experiences. It's all about attitude, and how we habitually think about our world. Most people probably fit somewhere in between the two extremes already mentioned. How does this come about? The thought patterns and habits of most people come about through their upbringing and other experiences in life. These processes are also thought to be at least partly genetically pre-programmed.

This approach to relaxation is all about examining how people think and what sorts of conversations they have with themselves, inside their heads. It focuses on what kind of 'inner dialogue' people have with themselves every day, and how that might be affecting levels of tension. We all have a kind of 'running commentary' going on in our heads, and it can often be negative and discouraging.

If a person's inner dialogue contains phrases such as 'I ought to get this done', 'I must not make a mistake', 'I know I can't cope with this', or 'What will people think?' they are making a rod for their own backs, and producing tension for themselves. It is so easy to slip into such habits in these pressured times. And this is not an illness of any kind. No, simply normal everyday patterns of thought and belief which encourage and exacerbate tension in the modern world. But how we think is not fixed for life. It can be changed.

Changing our thinking processes may make little difference to the big stresses of life, such as a bereavement, or if we live in an abusive relationship, but in the greyer areas of everyday life, our thoughts, or judgement of the situation can have a major impact on whether we experience tension or not. How we think in general can even be a significant cause of tension in the first place.

> *There is nothing either good or bad, but thinking makes it so.*
>
> William Shakespeare, playwright

How we think can affect us in two distinct ways:

▶ *It determines our reaction to a difficult situation, i.e. be crushed by it, or take it in our stride, or somewhere in between. It's not just about the situation we find ourselves in, it's about our* attitude *towards that situation.*
▶ *It can actually be the* cause of feeling tense *in the first place, e.g. expecting too much of ourselves, expecting too much of other people.*

Of course, in a complex world, these two can often work together and make things even worse for us.

Insight

Try to cultivate the true art of thinking for yourself, and believing in yourself. Its harvest will astound you.

CHANGING HOW YOU THINK

There have been many developments in this area since the 1960s, and these have given rise to a range of ways in which an individual may alter their thinking in order to reduce tension, and encourage relaxation. The general idea is to firstly become aware of the particular thinking styles and beliefs which may be causing a problem, and then take the appropriate steps to change these for the better. For many people, simply becoming aware of their established patterns of thought, and the impact these are having, can be enough to effect a substantial, effective and long-lasting change.

In 1962, Dr Albert Ellis began to explain how tension and stress may be the outcome of beliefs about the world held by an individual. He described these as 'irrational' beliefs in the sense that they are inflexible and dogmatic. They do not in any way represent a problem or an illness. Such beliefs are extremely common and entirely 'normal'.

Here are a few examples of mistaken beliefs taken from an extensive list. It is easy to see how holding even one of these beliefs can make life difficult, even in the absence of major problems:

- ▶ *Life should be fair.*
- ▶ *I should be able to do everything well.*
- ▶ *There should be a perfect solution for everything.*
- ▶ *I need everyone's approval for nearly everything I do.*
- ▶ *I should not make a mistake.*

Most of this thinking arises from growing up and living in a world where performance standards are set high, praise for a job well done is seen as encouraging an undesirable swollen head, and criticism of mistakes is never far away. All of this has produced low self-esteem and fear of failure in many people. If someone can become aware of and challenge these beliefs, their capacity for tension and stress should be reduced.

Most of these beliefs are therefore not undisputed truth, but have their roots in childhood and the culture around us. Ask yourself where these beliefs are written down or stated. Here is the same set of irrational or mistaken beliefs, along with ways of challenging them:

▶ *Life should be fair. (Says who? How could it be?)*
▶ *I should be able to do everything well. (Says who? Do you know anyone else who can?)*
▶ *There should be a perfect solution for everything. (Says who? How could there be?)*
▶ *I need everyone's approval for nearly everything I do. (Why? Says who? Is it possible anyway? You can't please all the people all the time.)*
▶ *I should not make a mistake. (Do you know anyone who doesn't make lots of them?)*

Many common tension-inducing beliefs include the words 'ought', 'should' or 'must'. These beliefs can impose high standards or 'personal rules' which produce frequent thoughts such as, 'I ought to do that gardening now' or, 'I must visit my mother today.' The standard is often set extremely high, with stress created because of this. Ask yourself who is setting these 'personal rules' and whether they are of too high a standard. Let yourself off the hook, and lower those standards if necessary.

▶ *I ought to have done that better. (Why? Says who?)*
▶ *I must cope with everything. (Why? Says who?)*
▶ *I should have done more. (Why? Says who?)*
▶ *I must not make a mistake. (Everyone does, why can't you?)*
▶ *I must get all of this done today. (Why? Says who?)*

Other beliefs and thoughts involve the words 'awful', 'terrible' or 'can't stand it', which usually exaggerate the reality of the situation:

▶ *I can't stand this. (You've stood things like this before, you can do it again. Is it really as bad as all that?)*
▶ *This is absolutely awful/terrible. (Some things are, but is this? What words have you left to use if something even worse happens?)*

Case study – Narinder

Narinder has consulted her GP because she feels tense all the time. She can't think of any reason for this as she has a nice house, three well-adjusted children and she gets on really well with her husband. When asked to describe her usual day, she says,

'I must get the shopping and housework done before lunchtime, so that I can get to work on time at one o'clock. I must leave the house tidy, so that I don't have to tidy it when I get back. I have this absolutely awful job at the supermarket, stacking shelves. I can't stand it, but we need the money. Then I rush home to cook dinner. I really ought to do more home cooking for the family, but trying to fit everything in is so terribly difficult. It isn't fair really, I try so hard, but I never seem to get it right. There must be some easy answer, because everybody else seems to cope better than I do.'

Much of Narinder's thinking is causing her unnecessary tension. She sets rules and expectations for herself which are impossible to meet, exaggerates situations, and is angry with life because it doesn't all work out the way she wants. It is quite common for much of this type of thinking to interlock together in a kind of 'ideology of life'. It is not being suggested that Narinder, or anybody, deliberately thinks in this way. These are thinking habits and beliefs which can creep up on anyone in today's hectic world where competition is endemic, and success and coping are so valued. It is therefore very common indeed.

So extensive is the possible range of irrational thinking that Ellis and his colleague Robert Harper were able to complete an entire book on the subject, called *A Guide to Rational Living*, and detailed therapy focusing on this is called Rational Emotive Therapy (RET). However, drawing your attention to some of the main areas and types of irrational thinking and their effects is enough for us here. Experience has shown this can have a striking and rapid effect on those who make use of it.

Try this – Examine your assumptions and beliefs

Here are some other 'mistaken assumptions and beliefs' about life. Think about these 'mistaken beliefs' and the 'correct' versions given alongside them.

Mistaken belief	'Correct' belief
I'm a failure if I make a mistake.	Absolutely everybody makes mistakes.
I should be happy all the time.	We all hope to be happy some of the time.
People must always like me.	Some people will like us, some won't.
I must always be successful.	Life has its ups and downs for all of us.
Life should be fair.	Life has never been fair, and never will be fair.

Thinking more positively

Professor Donald Meichenbaum, from Ontario, Canada, was one of the founders of this approach to thinking in the 1960s, and he also developed techniques based on the idea that our self-speech, the constant inner dialogue we have with ourselves, exerts considerable control over our behaviour. He also feels that people may have a very negative and self-defeating style of self-speech, which compounds already low self-esteem. This again is a common outcome of today's society and might include thoughts such as:

▶ *This is going to be really difficult, I don't think I can cope with it.*
▶ *I'll never manage this.*
▶ *I'm hopeless at this.*
▶ *I can't do this.*
▶ *Oh no, here we go again.*

This inner speech is therefore seen as a habit which can be changed, by using alternative phrases such as:

▶ *I've coped with this before, so I can do it again.*
▶ *I know I can do this if I try.*
▶ *I know I can do this quite well, and that should be good enough.*

POSITIVE THINKING STRATEGIES

▶ *Don't ignore the ordinary or good things that happen each day, as if they don't count for some reason. Take account of the bad side, but* don't dwell on it.
▶ *Take your mind off your problems as much as you can – they grow bigger the more you concentrate on them, but shrink into proportion when you think about something else.*
▶ *Get into the habit of thinking a* positive *thought frequently throughout the day – 'what a lovely blue sky' or, 'thank goodness I don't need to go out in that rain' – your thoughts are up to you, but keep them coming! It may sound silly, but it really works.*
▶ *Grow to like yourself. There will never be anyone else quite like you.*
▶ *Remember that many people, despite how they appear, are often as unsure of themselves as you are.*
▶ *Don't take part in 'negative conversation'. Change the subject to something more positive.*

- *Encourage friendships with people with positive thinking habits.*
- *Don't carry the world around on your shoulders. Give everybody else a share!*
- *Practise liking people.*
- *Count your blessings – old-fashioned, but still true!*

Insight

How do you see yourself? Think about that for a moment or two. Now focus on the fact that there will never be another you, so you are absolutely irreplaceable... warts and all... the mould was broken when you were made... How do you see yourself now? Any different?

Gaining a sense of control

In Chapter 4 of this book we saw how people differ in the extent to which they feel they can affect their situation, and have some control over what happens to them. Those with what was described as an 'external locus of control' feel they have very little control, and may be appraising their situation inappropriately and have taken none of the available steps to reduce their tension or stress.

This idea may lie at the heart of the difference between people who cave in, and those who flourish when faced with adversity. The former see the situation as beyond their control and give up, while the latter take control and put into place the required action to turn the situation around.

Try this – Taking back control

- *Remember that when things go wrong it's not always your fault – other people or the situation itself are just as likely to be to blame.*

(Contd)

> ▶ *You probably find some thoughts often slip into your mind like, 'I can't cope', 'I'm no good at this.' When this happens,* challenge *these thoughts. What evidence is there to support these thoughts – and what about the evidence against them? How would others view the situation? What would you say to a friend who felt that way?*
>
> ▶ *Avoid jumping to conclusions. We sometimes make decisions (usually wrongly) about a situation with no real evidence to support it, e.g. deciding a new friend doesn't like you because they refuse an invitation from you (when they probably have a valid reason for doing so). So, weigh up* all *the evidence before reaching decisions.*

Thinking errors

Our minds produce a constant train of thoughts, and these are seldom questioned. If we think a thought, we believe it must be a credible and reasonable thought, and there must be some truth in it. Not so. The currently very popular and effective 'cognitive behavioural therapy', or CBT, would certainly dispute this idea. Identifying our 'automatic' thoughts, and looking for the errors in them, makes up the main thrust of CBT. Dr Aaron Beck, recognized as the originator of cognitive therapy (the forerunner of CBT), first defined 'automatic thoughts' in the 1960s, as thoughts and images occurring involuntarily in the mind. Thoughts, behaviour and physiology were thought to be part of a single unified and interlinking system. Changing one affects the others. So, a person's thoughts will affect their physiology and their behaviour.

The innovative idea was that changing your thoughts could change your physiology and your behaviour. So, identifying the kind of thoughts which produced tension and anxiety, and changing them, became an idea worth pursuing. The kind of thinking which produced tension became known as thinking errors, or twisted thinking. Everyone has these thinking errors in their everyday thinking. It's all a matter of degree. Here are some of the most common. Some of these have been mentioned already.

Thinking error	How it affects your behaviour
Catastrophizing	Seeing an event or a person as more important than they are, far worse than they are, everything is out of proportion. Dwelling on the worst possible outcome of an event.
Black and white thinking	Thinking of people and events in black and white, good or bad, either/or, when really there are other options, and many shades of grey.
Emotional reasoning	Feeling that your mood reflects the way a situation really is, without considering any other evidence, e.g. your partner is late and this makes you feel rejected, but they may be late because of heavy traffic, the car breaking down, and so on.
Jumping to conclusions	Jumping to conclusions can happen in two main ways. 1 Fortune-telling, which means always anticipating that events or people will turn out badly. 2 Mind-reading, where we believe we know what others are thinking, without considering more plausible explanations for their behaviour.
Labelling	Deciding a person's characteristics based on one behaviour, or from limited experience of them, e.g. a person who makes one mistake is 'stupid'.
Mental filter	Not looking at people or situations as a whole. Concentrating entirely on the negative aspects, as if the positive side didn't matter at all.

(Contd)

Thinking error	How it affects your behaviour
Overgeneralization	Believing that if something didn't work out once, it will never work out, e.g. failing a driving test.
Personalization	Always blaming yourself for anything negative that happens, e.g. mistakes, accidents.
'Should', 'must' and 'ought' thinking	Placing demands on ourselves, usually excessive.

In order to work towards changing some of this distorted thinking, half the battle is just becoming aware of it, and how it might be affecting your behaviour. This can be a real eye-opener, and reduce tension and stress straight away. The second action you can take is to 'challenge' such thoughts whenever they occur. This process is best carried out slowly, one small step at a time.

Try this – Questioning and challenging unhelpful thoughts and beliefs

When you find yourself with unhelpful thoughts or beliefs, which make you tense, ask yourself the following questions, and answer them honestly:

1 *What is the evidence supporting this thought?*
2 *Who says it's true?*
3 *Is it written down somewhere that this is true?*
4 *What are the chances of it being true?*
5 *Is there an alternative explanation?*
6 *What is the evidence supporting the alternative explanation?*
7 *What would I tell a friend if they were in the same situation?*

You may also find it useful to give a rating of 0–100 for how much you believe the unhelpful thought before questioning it, and again afterwards, and see if you can make a difference.

Relax your mouth and eyes

You may be surprised to discover that whenever we are thinking, our eyes, mouth and tongue make very tiny movements which we are not aware of. They are tiny, but they will be there. As we have our everyday thoughts in our head, these are usually made up of words, and the muscles of speech make tiny movements. If we imagine we are doing something involving looking around, the muscles of sight will also make tiny movements. Test this out for yourself now. Read what to do first, then try it with your eyes closed.

Try this – Discovering tiny mouth and eye movements

While you are following these instructions, pay close attention to your eyes, mouth, lips and tongue.

1 *Imagine as clearly as you can that you are slowly walking into a room in a house. Any room in any house. You notice a large real fireplace on your right, and you look over at it. You look at the beautiful silver mirror over the fireplace, and then at the antique clock on the mantelpiece. Then you look at the coal bucket on the floor at the left-hand side of the fire.*
2 *Did you notice any eye movements as you were imagining this scene?*
3 *Now, imagine yourself sitting down in a comfy chair at the right-hand side of the fire, make yourself comfortable, and then imagine yourself saying. 'This is so relaxing, I could sit here for hours.'*
4 *Did you notice any movements of your tongue or mouth or lips as you imagined yourself speaking?*

Your eye movements can be more noticeable than those of your mouth and tongue, which tend to be tinier, but both come into action when we are thinking or imagining. So when you want to relax your mind, pay particular attention to relaxing the muscles of speech and sight. This can be surprisingly effective.

Using sounds

It is easy to understand that some sounds can be more relaxing than others. That said, these sounds can be particularly specific to an individual. What is relaxing and calming to one person, can be an annoying racket to someone else. There is a whole industry which has grown up around this area of relaxation, with CDs available with every conceivable sound you can think of. The more technologically advanced versions of these will be discussed later in Chapter 10. Sometimes the sounds and the music we find relaxing are very much tied to a previous happy or relaxing experience. The same applies to smells. The smell of freshly cut grass instantly transports me back to the sunshine and the open farm fields of my youth, with the hay newly cut. Aromatherapy builds on this idea, and will also be discussed later in Chapter 9. Many of the techniques for relaxing the mind given earlier in this chapter also use this principle.

Research, evidence and statistics

Instrumental and vocal music were found to be effective in reducing crying behaviours of newborns.

Lininger, 1987

Here are some examples of sounds which are commonly available on CD in music shops, gift shops, many garden centres and online.

You can usually 'try before you buy' to find out what you find relaxing, such as:

- *waves lapping on the seashore*
- *leaves blowing gently in the breeze*
- *sounds of a summer garden – gentle breeze, leaves, branches or long grass swaying, birds, buzzing bees, gurgling river*
- *birdsong, dolphin song, whale song*
- *a babbling brook*
- *a waterfall*
- *spring sounds – lambs bleating, birdsong, breeze, stream flowing.*

Research, evidence and statistics

According to Dr David Lewis (1986), in their desire to achieve mathematically perfect harmony, baroque composers succeeded in writing music where the frequency is precisely tuned to generate the beta/alpha/theta brainwave mixture we experience in 'relaxed awareness'.

MUSIC

Then there is music, and once again, this is subject to individual preferences. A number of recent studies have shown that music can do everything from slow the heart rate to increase endorphins. Popular music for relaxation includes *Air on the G String* by Bach, Beethoven's 'Pastoral' symphony, *Nocturne in G Minor* by Chopin and Handel's *Water Music*. Also easily available are other types of music which are thought to be relaxing:

- *Gregorian chants*
- *Baroque music (e.g. Handel, Bach, Vivaldi)*
- *New Age music*
- *any music where the tempo coincides with the average resting heart rate of 60 beats per minute*
- *pan pipes.*

BINAURAL BEATS

Earlier we learned how the alpha frequency of 8–12 Hz (1 Hz is one per second) is present in the brainwaves of individuals in a relaxed but aware state of mind. This frequency can usually only be obtained through meditation, or deep relaxation. It might seem that just listening to a sound with this frequency might be enough to create this state of mind. However, human ears can usually only hear between 20 and 20,000 Hz. Frequencies such as 8–12 Hz are simply too low for us.

Research, evidence and statistics

In 1839, German experimenter H. W. Dove found out that by playing two coherent sounds of very close, but not identical, frequencies into each ear, a third frequency (called the 'beat frequency' or 'binaural beat') could be experienced *inside* the mind.

This can be done by playing a pure tone of 400 Hz into the right ear, and a pure tone of 410 Hz to the left ear (using headphones). Inside the head, the difference between these two tones is actually what is experienced. So, a frequency of 10 Hz, or 10 per second is produced. This is equal to the alpha brainwave frequency, which brings about light relaxation and positive thinking.

Binaural beats in the delta (1–4 Hz) and theta (4–8 Hz) ranges have been associated with reports of relaxed, meditative and creative states (Hiew, 1995). Binaural beats in the alpha frequencies (8–12 Hz) have been shown to increase alpha brainwaves (Foster, 1990).

COMBINING SOUND AND IMAGERY

An individual choice of relaxing sounds combined with relaxing imagery can be extremely effective. A range of specialist DVDs is now easily available to suit most tastes. (Contact addresses are included in the 'Taking it further' section of this book.) (More on this in Chapter 10, which looks at how the Internet and modern technology can be used to provide this kind of relaxation experience. This chapter is complementary to the remainder of the book, so needn't be read if it is not of interest.)

Guided imagery

Of course, it is also possible and simple to produce imagery and sound completely from the imagination. This is called guided imagery, and can be done with the help of a CD describing the scene for you, or entirely using your own imagination to bring to mind calming images and sounds. See below for some examples of the latter.

Try this – Picture the scene

First, relax your body as much as possible, using any technique which works for you. Then close your eyes, and allow yourself to imagine that you are in one of the following settings. Build in as much detail and experience it as vividly as you can. Make the setting suit you. Hear the sounds, see the images, feel the sensations, smell the air around you, feel the sun on your skin.

It takes a little practice to get the full effect. Spend a minute or two in the setting. You can build this up gradually each time you practise to last as long as you want.

▶ *Lying or sitting by the ocean as the waves roll in... and... out, ... in... and ... out... feel the spray, hear the sounds, smell the salt in the air...*

(Contd)

- *Relaxing peacefully on a fluffy cloud, high in a blue sky, drifting along in the gentle breeze, and warmed by a bright shining sun...*
- *Walking or lying on a grassy mountaintop, tropical forest far beneath you, the morning rains just over, and warmed by the tropical sun... hear, see, feel, what can you touch?... grass underfoot?... between your fingers?... warm sun on your head...*
- *Standing or sitting under a shower of sparkling silver light... warm... gentle... and so refreshing... cleansing every part of your mind and soul... the shower is washing away all of your tension... all stress... freeing you from all cares and concerns... softly washing all of these away into the ground beneath your feet...*
- *Sitting or lying by a gurgling stream on a warm summer's morning... hear the birds singing in the trees and feel the grass beneath your feet... Or the water on your toes dipped in the clear, warm water...*
- *In your own special favourite place... where is it?... what are you doing?... sounds?...*

Make a note of which worked best for you.

Finally, highlight in some way anything which you felt would be helpful for you in this chapter (being aware of this is half the battle). If you haven't already done this, go back and do it now. A little bit at a time, try out some of the suggestions – but as usual, don't rush at it; a lifetime's habits take time to change.

Refer back to this chapter every so often to remind yourself of the various ideas, and to check out how things are changing in your thinking.

KEY POINTS

Look back over this chapter and choose the FOUR pieces of information you found to be most interesting or helpful. Write these here, or go back and underline or highlight them in some way.

1 ....

2 ....

3 ....

4 ....

Look back over this chapter and choose the FOUR practical suggestions you found to be most useful. Write these here, or go back and underline or highlight them in some way.

1 ....

2 ....

3 ....

4 ....

Which TWO techniques or suggestions from this chapter would you like to try out straight away?

Write these here, or go back and underline or highlight them in some way.

1 ....

2 ....

(Contd)

Which TWO techniques or suggestions from this chapter would you like to work towards using regularly?

Write these here, or go back and underline or highlight them in some way.

1 ....

2 ....

8

Relaxing mind and body together

In this chapter you will learn:
- *simple ways to meditate*
- *about mindfulness, t'ai chi, yoga, NLP and CBT*
- *how pets and animals can help you to relax.*

So far, ways of relaxing the body, and ways of relaxing the mind, separately, have been described. But many techniques for relaxing are much more holistic, aiming to relax the whole body, mind and self. This chapter will introduce some of the most common of these, from ancient to modern. Space doesn't allow for including all of them, as there are so many. If a particular method is of interest, and it is not included here, it is always best to check out the background of that particular school of thought before launching into it. It is also wise to check out a particular practitioner's training and experience before proceeding.

Insight

Lots of people are a bit scared of meditation because they think it's very hard to do, and they think they have to join a special religious or spiritual group to be able to give it a try. Neither of these concerns is true. It's simple to do, and you can try it right here, right now.

Meditation

Meditation in various forms has been used in numerous parts of the world throughout history, and has been found to be beneficial. Although it often has spiritual and religious associations, meditative techniques are themselves simple procedures, which can produce deep relaxation, and a very restful state of mind. Only methods which are not associated with any religion or cult will be discussed here, so that they will be suitable for all readers. However, if the other aspects of meditation are of interest, details of other reference materials are to be found in the 'Taking it further' section, at the end of the book.

> *During meditation, deep physiological relaxation, similar to deep sleep, occurs in a context of wakefulness.*
> Dr Patricia Carrington, Robert Wood Johnson Medical School,
> New Jersey, 1993

You don't have to wear anything special, or sit with legs crossed to meditate. Meditative techniques are typically carried out for 15–20 minutes every day, while seated comfortably, in quiet surroundings. Any relaxing music or sounds can be used in the background to allow a contemplative mood to be set before beginning to meditate, as well as during meditation to enhance the experience. This kind of music and sound was covered in Chapter 7.

Meditation has three main characteristics:

- ▶ *a quiet mind*
- ▶ *being in the here and now*
- ▶ *an 'altered state of consciousness'.*

This is nothing to be scared of, nor is it freaky or to do with taking drugs. This 'altered state of consciousness' just means it's different from the way we feel when we are going about our everyday business. It's a quieter, more centred, peaceful and grounded level, the sort of way you might feel out in the countryside on a sunny day, or out in the hills, or sitting on a quiet beach watching the waves lapping in and out. So, though it is an 'altered' state, it is still a 'normal' state. It is a state we are all capable of achieving.

In order to meditate, all that is required is to sit quietly, and concentrate entirely on a word, a sound, a picture or image, or other point of focus. Some methods need this to be attached to the breathing rhythm, others do not. If your attention wanders, all that is needed is to notice it quietly, and then simply and gently return to the point of focus. Like most relaxation techniques, some practice is likely to be needed, so have patience and give it time. It is well worth it.

Insight

I've always found that sitting quietly on a rock staring at the hills or the waves lapping on a quiet beach, has a very relaxing effect on my mind. I discovered much later that this is a simple form of meditation.

CHOOSE YOUR MANTRA OR MANDALA

The first important step is to select a special word or phrase, or a short poem or sound, or an image of some kind. A word, phrase or poem is known as a mantra; a picture or image is known as a mandala. Phrases in English, such as 'slow down' or 'let go' can also be used, and are sometimes called 'affirmations'. If you go to a meditation class, a list of these will be provided by the teacher for you to choose from. A mantra should sound resonant and soothing to the meditator. Likewise a picture or image should be calming and pleasing to the eye. If you have a faith or belief system which involves praying, you can pray while meditating, as an alternative to using a mantra, affirmation, or mandala.

Here are some short mantras and affirmations:

▶ *calm*
▶ *ahnam*
▶ *shi-rim*
▶ *one*

- *peaceful and quiet*
- *om*
- *ra-mah*
- *so-hum*
- *peace*
- *so-ham*
- *relax*
- *om... namah... shivaya... (sounded 'om numaa shivaa-yuh', it means 'I honour my own inner state' in Sanskrit).*

And here are some mandalas:

- *a flickering candle*
- *a loved one's face*
- *a favourite painting or picture*
- *a beautiful flower*
- *a tree in the breeze*
- *a sleeping animal.*

Try these – Meditation exercises

Option 1

1 *Choose one of the above mantras or affirmations.*
2 *Make yourself comfortable, sitting upright. You want to relax completely, but stay awake. Rest your arms and legs wherever feels comfortable for you.*
3 *Play some relaxing music or sounds if you find this helpful, and allow yourself to begin to relax and unwind slowly. Allow your mind and thinking to begin to slow down too. No pressure. Just let it happen in its own way and its own time.*
4 *Read what to do first (below), and then try it.*
5 *Begin by saying the chosen word, or words, out loud, stretching its sound in a long, slow and rhythmical fashion, for several repeats, then when you feel ready, whisper it, and then when it feels right, think it silently to yourself, and finally think it silently with your eyes closed.*
6 *If your attention wanders, don't be concerned, simply and gently return your thoughts to the point of focus.*

7   *Slowly build up from meditating in this way for a few*
    seconds at a session, to at most 15–20 minutes once or
    twice a day.

Option 2
Exactly as above, but in your own time, place the words only
on the outward breath.

Option 3
1   *Choose one of the above mandalas, or an image of your*
    own.
2   *Make yourself comfortable, sitting upright. You want to*
    relax completely, but stay awake. Rest your arms and legs
    wherever feels comfortable for you.
3   *Play some relaxing music or sounds if you find this helpful,*
    and allow yourself to begin to relax and unwind slowly.
    Allow your mind and thinking to begin to slow down too.
    No pressure. Just let it happen in its own way and its own
    time.
4   *Read what to do first (below), and then try it.*
5   *Begin by bringing your attention to your mandala. Gently*
    close your eyes when you feel ready. Don't force it, just let
    your attention slowly leave everything else behind, and begin
    to build your mandala in your mind's eye. Let that image
    slowly become stronger, clearer and more detailed. Focus
    completely on its every detail – textures, colours, shadows
    and light, movements.
6   *If your attention wanders, don't be concerned, simply and*
    gently return your thoughts to the point of focus.
7   *Slowly build up from meditating in this way for a few*
    seconds at a session, to at most 15–20 minutes once or twice
    a day.

MINI-MEDITATIONS

Dr Patricia Carrington suggests that 'mini-meditations' can also
work very effectively. This means that several shorter sessions of,
say, two or three minutes' duration, can be carried out several

times a day. This can be especially useful for active, busy people, and can be particularly good at keeping tension levels under control over a day. Break times at work, or while on the bus or train are good times for this.

COLOUR MEDITATION

As the name suggests, this technique uses breathing and colour to aid relaxation.

Try this – Colour meditation exercise

Choose whatever colour fits your mood or the one you wish to create.

- ▶ *Blues and greens are soothing, healing colours.*
- ▶ *Purple and violet are thoughtful and imaginative colours.*
- ▶ *Pure white is a cleansing and purifying colour.*
- ▶ *Yellow and orange are bright, energizing, happy colours.*

1 *Sit or stand comfortably, and let yourself begin to unwind.*
2 *Slowly breathe in and out, in your own time. Begin to imagine you are breathing in your colour along with your inward breath, and that it's going to fill your whole body.*
3 *Now, each time you breathe in, visualize the colour that you have chosen, streaming into your body with each breath, and spreading out from your lungs throughout your body, right to your fingertips, your toes, and up through your head to your scalp.*
4 *Keep doing this until you have achieved the state that you wish to create.*
5 *Enjoy this feeling for as long as you like.*

Take care: It is best to stick to one, or at most two, 15–20-minute sessions of meditation a day. More than this can begin to reverse its beneficial effects, or produce unwanted emotional experiences. With meditation, it is definitely a case of less being more.

Mindfulness

Mindfulness, or being mindful, is all about being aware of your present moment. You are not judging, reflecting or thinking. You are simply observing the moment in which you find yourself. It is similar to meditation. Moments are like a breath. Each breath is replaced by the next breath. You're there with no other purpose than being awake and aware of that moment. The here and now, the present moment is all that matters. The primary goal in mindfulness is maintaining a calm, non-judging awareness, allowing thoughts, feelings, and sensations to come and go without getting enmeshed in them. The past has gone, the future is yet to come, and what exists between them is the present moment, so live in that moment, savour it, and experience it and all its sensations fully. Try to notice your thoughts without being critical or judgemental of them.

The pioneer in the idea of mindfulness was Dr John Kabat-Zinn, Emeritus Professor of Medicine at the University of Massachusetts, who began his work on the subject relatively recently, in the 1980s.

Try these – mindfulness exercises

Mindfulness and your day

Experience everything you do each day. Live in and inhabit the moment. Don't miss a thing. Feel the water from the shower as it touches your skin, the towel as it dries you off, your bare feet on the bathroom floor. As you hang out the washing, feel each peg in your hand, and the fabric in the shirt, and in each towel. Focus on the breeze on your cheek, the sun on the top of your head. In the office, feel each finger's touch on the keyboard, your hand on the mouse, your feelings, your voice and your breathing as you chat to colleagues at lunchtime. Savour your meals: focus on the textures, the flavours, the aroma, the colours. Feel the touch of the spoon on your hand. As you travel home on the train, notice each feeling, each reaction to those around you, and notice the world passing by the window – trees, people's back gardens, life going on inside their windows. Notice your touch on the front door handle as you arrive home. Feel the warmth of the water as you do the washing-up. Focus on the gestures, the facial expressions and the stories of the friend you drop in to see. Then at home again, see the textures and colours of the late evening sky, before tumbling into bed, and experiencing the sensation of the smooth, fresh cotton sheets on your toes, and the soft fragrant pillow under your head.

Mindfulness and walking

Use this technique anywhere you're walking – in a tranquil forest, in the city, or at the shops. Slow down the pace of walking so that you can focus on each movement of your head, body, arms, legs, feet and toes. Don't focus on a particular destination. Just be in the moment, wherever you are. Concentrate on your legs and feet, as you lift each foot, move your leg forward and place your foot on the ground. Focus on what it feels like in the sole of your foot, what it sounds like. What are your toes doing? What are your arms doing? Swinging gently in the rhythm of your walking, or holding a bag, or hands in pockets, or maybe fingers cosy inside gloves. Feel your fingers touching the inside of the glove, or the inside of your pocket, or grasping the textured strap of a bag. Are you wearing a hat or a scarf? Or can you feel the breeze on your hair or your ears? What can you hear? What can you see just close by? What are you feeling?

Mindfulness and breathing
As you go about your everyday activities, simply concentrate on breathing in through your nose and out through your mouth, and breath mainly with your abdomen, not your chest. Focus clearly on the sound, the movement and the rhythm of your breathing. Live completely in the present moment.

Mindfulness, music and sounds
Select any music or recorded sound which encourages relaxation and calming for you. To add the mindfulness dimension, really focus on each sound or each note, focus on the type of sound, the instrument, its depth, its tone, its volume, its pitch, and so on. Focus on the changes and variations in the sound. Really experience the feelings, the emotions, the sensations which the music is producing in you 'here and now' as you are listening.

Insight

The idea of Mindfulness is a very recent development, but I feel it's been one of the best, and has huge potential.

Yoga

Yoga encourages mental calmness and body awareness through concentrating on various specific movements and poses. The word yoga means 'union' in Sanskrit, which is the language of ancient India where yoga originated. The name relates to the union between the mind, body and spirit, which the full practice of yoga can bring. What is commonly referred to as 'yoga' in the West can be more accurately described by the Sanskrit word 'asana', which refers to the part of yoga involving the practice of physical postures or poses. Asana is only one of the eight aspects of yoga, the majority of which are more concerned with mental and spiritual well-being than physical activity. In the West, however, the words asana and yoga are often used interchangeably.

POSES

Many people think that yoga is just about stretching the body. And while stretching is certainly involved, yoga is really about creating balance through developing both strength and flexibility. This is done using a wide range of special poses or postures, each of which has specific physical benefits. They often have animal names such as the Cobra, the Cat, or the Lion.

CLASSES

In addition to practising the poses, yoga classes in the West may also include breathing exercises, or basic meditation, and they often finish with a session of Total Relaxation. The variety and amount of each will depend on the individual teacher and their yoga tradition. A yoga class at a gym will be more focused on the physical benefits of yoga, while one at a specialist yoga centre may concentrate more on the spiritual side.

BREATHING EXERCISES

Yoga breathing exercises are called 'Pranayama' in Sanskrit, and can be done alongside yoga poses or just while sitting quietly. Here is one of the most well-known yoga breathing exercises. It is usually found to be balancing, relaxing and calming.

Try this – Alternate nostril breathing

1 *Sit in a comfortable, upright position.*
2 *Using your right hand, bring your thumb to the right side of your nose and your index finger to the left side.*
3 *Now gently close off your right nostril with your thumb.*

4   Inhale through your left nostril, in your own time.
5   Now close off your left nostril with your index finger, allowing your right nostril to open again.
6   Exhale through your right nostril in your own time.
7   Inhale through your right nostril.
8   Close off your right nostril with your thumb, allowing your left nostril to open.
9   Exhale through your left nostril.
10 Inhale through your left nostril.
11 Continue alternating between five and ten times.

T'ai chi

T'ai chi (pronounced 'ty chee') is often described as 'meditation in motion'. It was created based on nature and harmony, and consists of a sequence of graceful flowing movements and deep breathing exercises designed to encourage relaxation, inner calm and mental balance. T'ai chi aims to achieve harmony with nature and the balance of mental serenity and physical strength. It is much easier to learn by attending a class or group, with an experienced teacher.

It originated in China as a martial art, although its full history is unclear, and appears to have been in use in the seventeenth century. Several styles of t'ai chi have developed but the most commonly seen is the t'ai chi which is non-competitive, and involves the slow and gentle exercises taught in most classes. The movements are performed slowly with relaxed muscles and the mind focused on each step. There are more than 100 possible movements and positions, and you can find several that you like and stick with those, or explore the full range. They are not intended to be strenuous or muscle building, but to gently exercise the body, calm the mind and stimulate the internal organs. T'ai chi is similar to yoga in that it concentrates on various specific movements and poses.

T'ai chi followers believe that the slow, rhythmic movements of the body help calm the mind, and relax the muscles and nervous system.

They believe that if practised daily, this can have a lasting effect. And t'ai chi, as one of the most powerful mind–body exercises, teaches the student to be aware of the intrinsic energy from which they can perceive greater self-control and empowerment.

T'ai chi means 'supreme ultimate' and most students notice a feeling of relaxation following the classes, which in time can become a more profound feeling of calm and peace. As a non-physical form of exercise t'ai chi is suitable for any age. As well as producing relaxation, the postures and movements involved have been shown to improve muscle tone, flexibility and balance.

The 'typical' t'ai chi class will consist of a short warm-up routine of stretches, a number of breathing exercises, and practice of one or more 'forms' – the sets of movements which most people think of when they consider t'ai chi. These forms can be hundreds of movements long and take many years to learn fully.

Petting an animal

It is now well documented that stroking a friendly cat or dog has a relaxing effect and can even lower blood pressure. Further research now shows that if the pet is your companion, this effect is reinforced.

Research, evidence and statistics

In a study of 100 women conducted at the State University of New York at Buffalo, researchers found that those who owned a dog had lower blood pressure than those who didn't. Petting an animal for just a couple of minutes helps relieve stress.

Michael Castleman

It's not just cats and dogs which can have this relaxing effect. Any pet companion will have the same positive effect: rabbit, budgie, hamster, and so on. Even watching fish swimming around a fish tank has been shown to have beneficial effects, including relaxation and lowered blood pressure. Although for most people the idea of companionship and relaxation provided by pets conjures up an image of a furry domestic animal, an interesting study by Eddy (1996) provides evidence that attachment to any species is likely to elicit favourable physiological responses in pet owners. Eddy studied relaxation responses and reported that for a snake owner, stroking a pet snake produced greater reductions in blood pressure than stroking a cat or a dog.

Many people find horse-riding particularly relaxing. There is the close contact with the animal, but there is also fresh air, exercise, and the relaxing effect of the slow rhythmic movement of the horse. In order to ride well, the body and mind must be relaxed, and a riding teacher will take time to explain to all new riders how to be fully relaxed. Horse-riding also brings about increased self-confidence and improved self-esteem. All of these benefits have been put to good use for many years by professionals such as occupational therapists and charitable groups seeking to help people with disabilities, such as cerebral palsy. There are various terms used for this, such as 'equine movement therapy', or 'hippotherapy', or the more familiar 'riding for the disabled', with over 500 centres providing this activity in the UK, and another 600 involved in the USA.

'Pet therapy' or 'Therapets' are now widely used in nursing homes, prisons and long-stay hospitals to reduce stress and depression, as well as encouraging residents to come out of themselves and engage with the animal. All sorts of animals are involved in this, including sheep, lambs, rabbits, donkeys and chickens. In some cases, a very friendly, docile donkey is taken right into the care home sitting room, and even into residents' rooms. Some city farms run regular interactive sessions for children with special needs, with the tactile experience especially meaningful for those with a sight impairment.

However, think carefully before getting a pet mainly for relaxation purposes. Owning a pet brings with it many responsibilities, expenses and extra work. And where you live may not be suitable, or your lease may ban pet ownership. On the benefits side, owning a dog will mean regular walks in the fresh air, and chatting to others similarly engaged. All of these also have a relaxing effect. It's not a decision to be taken lightly whatever your reason for having a pet.

Research, evidence and statistics

We have demonstrated that petting a dog, with whom a companion bond has been established, has a positive cardiovascular effect, with an effect that parallels that of quiet reading.

Baun, Bergstrom, Langston, & Thoma, 1984

Qigong

Qigong (pronounced chee-gong) means 'the skill of attracting vital energy'. It is an ancient art which combines movement and meditation, and makes use of visualizations to strengthen the connection of body and mind. Regular practice can bring balance, and bring together mind, body and spirit, producing peace and tranquillity.

Qigong is a 5,000-year-old Chinese practice designed to promote the flow of 'chi', the vital life force that flows throughout the body, regulating its functions. There are two main kinds of qigong, called internal and external. Internal qigong is much like meditation, with visualizations in order to guide the energy. External qigong includes movement to accompany the meditation.

Insight

The next two topics are NLP and CBT – don't be put off because of the wordy names and the initialisms. They have much to offer you.

Neurolinguistic programming

Neurolinguistic programming, or NLP for short, has only been introduced relatively recently and has grown rapidly ever since. It was first defined by Dr Richard Bandler (a mathematician), and John Grinder (an Associate Professor of Linguistics) working together at the University of California in the early 1970s. Since then, it has developed into a powerful body of information about how the human mind works. You are likely to find many different descriptions of NLP, as it is a very broad school. Neurolinguistic programming describes the fundamental dynamics between mind (neuro) and language (linguistic) and how their interplay affects our body and behaviour (programming). In essence, it aims to allow us to become aware of, and understand, our habitual patterns of thought and behaviour, and to change these for the better. These patterns are usually laid down and established in childhood, and affect our whole way of living and interacting with others, without us realizing this. Being tense or relaxed is clearly going to be part of this pattern, meaning that NLP can have a relaxing effect on body and mind, and even on your core being. It can even extend the horizons of our thinking and behaviour.

In practice, NLP offers a wide range of methods and models to help us understand how people think, behave and change. NLP also provides the skills needed to define and achieve our outcomes or goals, and also gives a heightened awareness of our senses, and how these can affect our thinking patterns. You use words to describe your thoughts. If your thoughts (internal representations) are mainly pictures, then you will tend to use more visual words when describing your thoughts. Similarly for the other senses.

So, for example, some people tend to use words and phrases related to touch, such as 'get to grips with' or 'hold on a moment'. These are referred to as 'kinaesthetic'. Similarly, you may be more 'olfactory' and use phrases like 'coming up roses', or be more visual or auditory and use phrases like 'from my point of view' or 'turning a deaf ear'. If your thoughts are based on logic or making sense of something, you may tend to use words that reflect the logic of your thinking; this is called 'auditory digital' thinking and speaking.

Here are some more examples.

Sense	Examples of words	Examples of phrases
Visual (sight)	Focus, insight, perspective, illustrate, see, look, notice, picture, view, illuminate.	The future looks bright. My point of view. Look forward to. Tunnel vision. I see what you mean.

Auditory (hearing)	Speechless, listen, harmony, hear, tell, sound.	Sounds good. Speak your mind. Loud and clear. Rings a bell. On another note. Voice an opinion. Sound you out.
Auditory digital (logic)	Understand, think, process, question, detail, describe, know, learn, logical.	Figure things out. Make sense of. Word for word. Without a doubt. Chances are.
Kinaesthetic (touch/feel)	Touch, feel, grasp, soft, hard, warm, cold, smooth, rough.	Grasp the nettle. Touch base. Get hold of. Get a handle on. Hang in there. Smooth operator.
Gustatory (taste)	Bitter, sweet, taste, flavour, appetite, food, diet, meal.	A taste for it. Sugar and spice. A bitter experience. Food for thought. Make a meal of it.
Olfactory (smell)	Aroma, fragrant, perfume, smell, pungent, nose, odour.	Sweet smell of success. A nose for it. Smell a rat. Smelling of roses.

Language affects how we think, behave and respond, so it's easy to understand why this might be important. In relationships, if one person tends to think mainly in a visual way, while the other thinks mainly in a kinaesthetic way, problems and tensions may be created. Raising awareness of these differences is thought to enhance relationships and smooth running at home and at work.

NLP also suggests what our eye movements say about our thinking while we are talking or listening. For example, when we look up, or into the middle distance, we are visualizing; downward and we are accessing feelings. We move our eyes sideways to the right or left when we hear sounds internally. Looking down to our left usually suggests internal dialogue is going on. It's important to be aware that these are eye movements, not whole head movements, though some head movement can be involved too. What this means is that, taking all this in reverse, if you want to help yourself to access your feelings, then looking downwards can help; looking upwards, or into the middle distance, will make it easier to visualize. Visualization is an important part of many of the techniques covered in this book.

NLP is something you can easily learn about and use for yourself by reading up on it. Suggested reading is provided in the 'Taking it further' section at the end of the book. Heightening awareness is a huge part of NLP, so simply reading more about it will make inroads into the process. To take it further than this, an NLP coach or counsellor would be needed and, as mentioned already, check out such a person's background before proceeding with this, as there is currently no official body which oversees this area of work.

Cognitive behavioural therapy

As its name implies, CBT combines two very effective forms of therapy: cognitive therapy and behaviour therapy, both of which have been touched on in previous chapters.

Cognitive therapy improves understanding of how certain patterns of thinking can be causing and maintaining symptoms, such as anxiety, tension or depression. So-called 'distorted thinking' can influence feelings, emotions and behaviour, and can lead us to behave and feel depressed, anxious, tense or angry. Challenging and changing these distorted thoughts can provide improved control over behaviours and feelings.

Behaviour therapy aims to weaken the connection between situations and unhelpful reactions to them, such as tension or anxiety.

Both of these therapies together can offer powerful tools, which can increase understanding, and change and control the way you think, feel and behave. All of this has clear links to being able to relax. CBT has been rigorously tested, with study after study showing CBT to be very effective.

Many of the techniques already covered in this book have been based on CBT, so some aspects of CBT have already been explained and described. In particular, those CBT techniques which can easily be used independently have been covered already. A description of other important aspects of CBT will now follow. To take this further, it would be advisable to seek a qualified and experienced therapist (contact details are provided in the 'Taking it further' section at the end of the book).

FUNDAMENTAL ASPECTS OF CBT

► *Cognitive behavioural therapy is based on the idea that it is our thoughts which cause our feelings and behaviours, not external things, like people, situations and events. The benefit of this idea is that we can change the way we think, so we can change how we feel and behave for the better, even if the situation itself does not change.*
► *CBT is teamwork, between the therapist and the client. The therapist seeks to learn what the client wants out of life, and then helps the client achieve this.*
► *The therapist's role is to listen, teach and encourage, while the client's role is to express their concerns, learn, and implement that learning.*
► *The client changes because they learn how to think differently and they act on that learning.*
► *CBT does not tell people how they should feel.*
► *Therapists ask questions, and encourage their clients to ask questions of themselves, like, 'How do I really know that*

those people are laughing at me?', 'Could they be laughing about something else?'

▶ *CBT is structured and directive. Therapists have a specific plan for each session.*

▶ *Specific techniques/concepts are taught during each session.*

▶ *The client is not told what their goals 'should' be.*

▶ *CBT is directive in the sense that clients are shown how to think and behave in ways which help them to reach their goals.*

▶ *CBT therapists do not tell their clients what to do; rather, they teach their clients how to do.*

▶ *CBT is based on the scientifically supported assumption that most emotional and behavioural reactions are learned. Therefore, the goal of therapy is to help clients unlearn their unwanted reactions and to learn a new way of reacting.*

▶ *CBT has nothing to do with 'just talking'. People can 'just talk' with anyone.*

▶ *CBT involves giving clients 'homework' to do between sessions – reading, completing diaries or practising the techniques learned.*

KEY POINTS

Look back over this chapter and choose the FOUR pieces of information you found to be most interesting or helpful. Write these here, or go back and underline or highlight them in some way.

1 ....

2 ....

3 ....

4 ....

Look back over this chapter and choose the FOUR practical suggestions you found to be most useful. Write these here, or go back and underline or highlight them in some way.

1 ....

2 ....

3 ....

4 ....

Which TWO techniques or suggestions from this chapter would you like to try out straight away?

Write these here, or go back and underline or highlight them in some way.

1 ....

2 ....

(Contd)

Which TWO techniques or suggestions from this chapter would you like to work towards using regularly?

Write these here, or go back and underline or highlight them in some way.

1 ....

2 ....

9

More alternative and complementary therapies

In this chapter you will learn:
- *about a range of types of massage*
- *the benefits of acupuncture, reiki, biofeedback, EFT and other therapies*
- *what to look for in alternative and complementary therapies*
- *self-help methods for suitable therapies.*

In the last chapter, a range of techniques which were directed at the whole mind, body and self were introduced. Some of these would fall into the category of alternative and complementary therapies (ACTs). A very broad and varied range of ACTs is available, and this chapter will look at some of those which is more focused on a particular part, or a particular function of the body or mind. Almost all ACTs can have a relaxing aspect to them, even if it's just because quality time is being spent doing something enjoyable or peaceful in supportive and interesting company. It's really all about finding which can work for you, fall within your budget, and fit easily into your life.

In this chapter, some of the most common forms of ACTs are described, which also have research or strong anecdotal evidence suggesting that they directly encourage relaxation. Wherever possible, self-help techniques are also included as a taster. If you do decide to try out any of these therapies, or any other, it's important to make sure the therapist or practitioner is fully qualified in their particular field. Going on personal recommendation, or contacting only practitioners who are members of an established and recognized professional group, are good strategies.

Massage

Massage therapy originated in China about 2,000 years ago, primarily associated with improving health. From there it travelled to India and then to ancient Greece, Rome and on to Persia. Now massage has become popular for loosening muscles and relaxing tension. Although several special instruments have been developed to use in massage, the most satisfying massage is still that administered using the hands. Perhaps it's more relaxing because of the human contact. But whether it's a full body massage that can last for an hour or two, or a quick back rub given by someone you love, a massage is a great way to relax.

During a massage, a therapist manipulates the body's soft tissues, that is, the muscles, skin and tendons, using fingertips and hands. Massage can be performed by several types of health care professional, such as a physiotherapist, occupational therapist or massage therapist. Many versions of massage exist, and they are performed in a variety of settings, from Indian head massage, to shiatsu, to aromatherapy massage, Swedish massage, hot stone massage, chair massage and many, many more. Most people feel calm and relaxed after a treatment. Occasionally, people experience mild temporary aching in the muscles for a day or so afterwards.

It would be impossible to cover every type of massage here, so some basic information is given, to give a broad picture of what this technique has to offer. If you want to find out more, contact details can be found at the back of the book.

PRECAUTIONS

There are some thoughts and precautions worth mentioning before explaining more on this topic.

- Massage for relaxation shouldn't hurt – occasionally there may be mild aching at first as pressure is applied over 'knots' and other areas of muscle tension.
- Don't eat a heavy meal just before a full body massage.
- Massage in pregnant women should be done by massage therapists who are certificated in pregnancy massage.
- If you are pregnant, or if you have heart disease, you should check with your GP first.
- You shouldn't have a massage in any area of the body with infectious skin disease, a rash, open wound/s, abnormal sensitivity to touch, varicose veins or bruising.
- You usually shouldn't have a full body massage if you have inflammatory conditions, varicose veins, tumours or cysts, or if you have fever, cardiovascular/circulatory conditions, blood clots, diabetes or cancer, or if you've just had surgery, chemotherapy or radiation treatment (unless it has been recommended by your doctor).

WHAT YOU CAN EXPECT DURING A MASSAGE

- No matter what kind of massage you choose, you should feel calm and relaxed during and after your massage.
- Your massage therapist will ask what you want from your massage. Massage therapists will also want to know about any medical conditions you may have, so they can decide if massage is safe for you or how to make it safer.
- You'll be asked to remove some of your clothes, depending on whether you are having a full or partial massage. You will be given privacy to do this, and a robe or a towel will be provided to cover yourself if necessary. A good massage therapist will protect your modesty and keep you covered as much as possible throughout the massage.
- Most massages will require you to lie on a padded table. Pillows or bolsters might be used to position you comfortably. Music usually plays softly while you're massaged.
- Some massage therapists use oils or lotions to reduce friction while massaging your body, or to provide a relaxing perfume, as in aromatherapy.

▶ *You shouldn't feel discomfort in a relaxation massage. If you feel too much pressure is being used, ask the therapist to lighten the pressure. Your massage therapist should welcome feedback from you on how best to massage you.*

▶ *Allow at least an hour. Most table massages take about an hour, though some can be up to 90 minutes long.*

ON-SITE MASSAGE IN THE WORKPLACE

Many employers are now providing massage in the workplace as an aid to relieving tension and stress, sometimes at break times, and sometimes during working hours. Every work environment is a bit different, so this can be done in several ways. For example, chair massage may be given in a private room or corner of the office. This is done with the employee fully clothed, seated upright using a special chair, sometimes with the head leaning forward resting on a special support. The massage would be done on the shoulders, neck and upper back, and would last 10–15 minutes. Similar massages are now on offer in most airport departure lounges. Alternatively, neck and shoulder massage is sometimes now provided during working hours and fully clothed at the employee's desk. In some workplaces, the employee lies down on a flat massage plinth partially clothed, exposing the back and shoulders for a 20–30-minute session. This would have to take place in a private space with blinds and door shut.

Try this – DIY relaxation massage

If you want to try this out on yourself or on someone else, either on the whole body or just a part of it, here's what to do. It's great for aching shoulders or neck, or a tension headache. Doing your own massage isn't as nice as having someone else do it, but it still makes you feel more relaxed.

Full body

1 *Plan to be undisturbed for an hour or longer. Choose a time when you won't be disturbed.*

2 *Play some music or sounds which help you relax.*

3 *Have clothes on or clothes off depending on preference.*

4 *Use lotion or oil on bare skin, or dry hands on clothing.*

5 *Do the massage on the floor or in bed, not too warm, not too cold.*

6 *Note that normal muscle tone feels firm yet soft.*

7 *Use easy, non-tiring massage strokes. Slow, long, gliding strokes, using light to medium pressure and flat fingers, are for relaxation and calming. If the pressure used could just crush a ripe grape under your fingers, it's about right.*

8 *Start with your feet and progress upwards, or start with your head and progress downwards.*

9 *If working on yourself, adjust your position to be able to reach and work on areas without getting tired. For example, recline (leaning against the headboard or wall) when massaging feet. Sit up to do legs, lie on your side to massage the hips. Sit up again to do arms, and lie down on your back to massage the neck and face. The back is hard to reach, so just do the best you can. Whatever area you are working with, position yourself in a way that is comfortable for you.*

10 *Relax and enjoy the feeling.*

Single area

Massage can be used on any area, but a foot massage or hand massage can help relax your entire body or help induce sleep. A face or scalp massage or, if working on someone else, shoulders and neck, or back, can also be very relaxing, and remove tension in a particular area.

1 *Allow ten to 20 minutes when you won't be disturbed.*

2 *Play some music or sounds which help you relax.*

3 *Remove relevant clothing if preferred.*

4 *On skin, use dry hands or a little lotion or oil. Dry hands on clothing.*

5 *Note that normal muscle tone feels firm yet soft.*

(Contd)

6 *Feet or hands: work the whole foot or hand, then the fingers or toes. Face: work upwards or downwards. Scalp: back to front or the reverse. Shoulders and neck: work from centre back of the neck, slowly radiating outwards till whole area is covered.*

7 *Start slowly with gentle, short, broad strokes, with flattened fingers, to warm up the whole area to be massaged.*

8 *Now, still with flat fingers, use slow, gliding strokes, and light to medium pressure to release tension, and to relax and calm. If the pressure used could just crush a ripe grape under your fingers, it's about right.*

9 *Relax and enjoy the feeling.*

Reflexology

The practice of reflexology has come and gone throughout history, and across the world, with evidence of similar practices being traced back as far as China and India in the third millennium BC, and Japan around 700 BC. Reflexology in the twenty-first century is the physical act of applying pressure to the feet and hands with specific thumb, finger and hand techniques without the use of oil or lotion. It has become a very popular alternative therapy over the past few decades, and for those who enjoy someone working with their feet, it promotes relaxation, and soothes tired feet.

On this much, everyone would agree. Whether you agree with the more detailed practice and explanation of reflexology and how it works is a personal choice. However, it will still work, and make you more relaxed, whatever your beliefs. For the purposes of this book, we'll stick with the baseline position that it does encourage relaxation in those who don't object to someone working with their feet.

It can easily be taken further from here, for those who are interested. For example, most reflexologists work on a system of zones and reflex areas on the feet and hands with a premise that such work effects a physical change to the body, and that these changes are connected in some way to specific areas of the feet and hands being worked on. So, working on the base of the big toe would produce a change in the back of the neck, and work in the centre of the ball of the foot would relieve nervous tension throughout the body.

Reflexology can be done without a therapist's help, by using various types of balls, textured surfaces, or rollers either between the hands or by rolling the feet over them on the floor, or standing on them in the shower. It is probably best experienced with the help of a qualified therapist.

A REFLEXOLOGY SESSION

▶ *Reflexology sessions in general last from 30 minutes to an hour. It is a clothed session with only the removal of shoes and socks as a requirement.*
▶ *You will be seated in a comfortable chair or sometimes lie comfortably on a table.*
▶ *Reflexologists use pressure, stretch and movement to work through both feet methodically.*
▶ *Sometimes reflexology is done using pleasantly scented oils, sometimes dry.*
▶ *The reflexologist should work within your comfort zone, with a moderate level of pressure, but not enough to cause discomfort. The pressure has to be firm enough not to tickle the feet.*
▶ *You can talk with the therapist during treatment if you want to, but keep this light so as not to detract from the relaxing effects. There may be relaxing music or sounds playing.*
▶ *You should enjoy the session, and feel relaxed at the end of it. How long this relaxation lasts is a good indicator of how effective it has been for you.*

Insight

We all benefit from a little variety. So even if you don't want to use an ACT regularly for relaxation, or find it too expensive, it's nice to give one a try for a change, or for a special treat.

Acupuncture

Acupuncture is the ancient art of inserting small needles into certain acupuncture points in the body. Acupuncture originated in China 5,000 years ago, but there are also Japanese, Tibetan and Korean versions. By inserting these needles into the acupuncture points, it is believed that certain pains and diseases can be alleviated. But, acupuncture can also be calming and relaxing.

There does seem to be substantial evidence of acupuncture being effective for many people, and for a number of conditions. And there is evidence of acupuncture producing a relaxation effect.

Research, evidence and statistics

- ▶ *A study of acupuncture, which took place in Germany, appeared in the* British Medical Journal *in 2005. Researchers Melchert, Streng and Hoppe studied 270 men and women who had regular tension headaches and received acupuncture treatment. A statistically significant number of patients experienced an improvement in their headaches, and this effect lasted several months after treatment.*
- ▶ *Professor Pierre Huard of the Medical Faculty of Paris states that acupuncture is equivalent to the effect of tranquilizers, and its action is quick and lasting.*
- ▶ *Research published in the* Traditional Chinese Medical Journal *has indicated that acupuncture can cause a decrease in delta brainwaves and an increase in the fast alpha brainwaves that are associated with relaxation.*

The basis of acupuncture is the idea that the body has an energy force running throughout it. This energy force is known as Qi (roughly pronounced 'chee'). Qi travels throughout the body along 'meridians' or special pathways. The meridians (or channels) are mirrored on both sides of the body, and 14 main meridians run vertically up and down the surface of the body. The acupuncture points are specific locations where the meridians come to the surface of the skin, and are easily accessible by acupuncture. The connections between them ensure that there is an even circulation of Qi. Energy constantly flows up and down these pathways, and this can be out of balance. Acupuncture is said to restore the balance.

As with other therapies, there is much in the way of explanation and details of this process, but for this book, there is no need to go beyond this basic starting point, unless you have a particular interest. After all, there's no need to have a complex understanding or knowledge of pharmaceuticals, in order to take paracetamol for a bad back. The important point is that for some people, who are comfortable with the idea of acupuncture, this can be an effective way to relax.

Acupuncture is not really something you can do for yourself, so if you are interested, the usual guidance applies about finding a qualified practitioner.

That said, there is an alternative to acupuncture which doesn't use needles. This is called acupressure, and this process stimulates the same points as acupuncture, but with fingers instead of needles. Reflexology could be considered an example of this.

Try this – Self-acupressure

Dr Michael Reed Gach, director of the Acupressure Institute in Berkeley, CA, recommends the following:

1 *Begin by sitting or lying comfortably.*
2 *Using the flat of one or two fingers, apply firm, steady pressure on one of the following three points for two to three minutes. The pressure may cause a mild aching sensation, but not pain.*
(Contd)

> ▷ The Third Eye – located between the eyebrows, in the
>   indentation where the bridge of the nose meets the
>   forehead.
> ▷ The Heavenly Pillar – on the back of the neck slightly
>   below the base of the skull, about half an inch to the left
>   or right of the spine.
> ▷ The Heavenly Rejuvenation – half an inch below the top
>   of each shoulder, midway between the base of the neck
>   and the outside of the shoulder blade.
>
> 3 Now repeat for the other two points, if you want to.

AN ACUPUNCTURE SESSION

▶ When you visit the practitioner for the first time, you'll be
  asked questions about your general health and any conditions
  from which you suffer.
▶ When ready to begin the treatment, you will lie down and the
  skin on the areas where the needles will be inserted will be
  sterilized using a wipe.
▶ Each needle is hair thin, and sterile, and only inserted between
  three and five millimetres into the skin. You normally will not
  feel any pain, but many patients say they experience a feeling
  of tingling and relaxation while the needles are in place.
▶ The practitioner will leave the needles in the skin for between
  15 and 20 minutes, so it is important that you remain still to
  keep from hurting yourself.

THE SCIENTIFIC APPROACH TO ACUPUNCTURE

From a scientific point of view, it is still not clear exactly how
acupuncture works, but there are a number of theories:

▶ Acupuncture may stimulate the secretion of endorphins in the
  body (explained earlier in the book).
▶ Neurotransmitter levels, such as serotonin (see earlier in the
  book), are affected by acupuncture.
▶ Acupuncture may have the effect of constricting or dilating
  blood vessels. This may be caused by the body's release of
  'vasodilators' (such as histamine), in response to acupuncture.

Insight

'Biofeedback', the topic in the next section, is much more straightforward than it sounds, and is very popular with those who try it.

Biofeedback

There are various forms of biofeedback, which is not as complex and scientific as it sounds. It simply involves giving some form of immediate 'biological feedback' to a person, as to whether they are relaxing or not. For example, this can be feedback on skin temperature, breathing or heart rate, or brain, muscle or skin activity.

Techniques and equipment have been introduced which involve giving you feedback on your reducing tension in the form of a moving pointer, or as a sound or a light display, or in some other way. This lets you know immediately that what you are doing is actually relaxing you, so this encourages you to continue what you were doing and the process of relaxation will continue.

Many people particularly enjoy this method, and enjoy watching the pointer fall or the sound level reduce on the particular equipment they are using. A wide range of equipment of this kind is available, varying from a few pounds to much more expensive, from the simple stress dot to devices producing feedback in the form of colour change, sound or light, to monitors analysing brainwave activity, to highly entertaining computer-based activities. These will be covered in Chapter 10. You can use biofeedback for yourself, without a therapist, and this is its most common way of being used. There are also a few therapists offering biofeedback therapy if you prefer to try it that way, or you may sometimes find a GP, nurse practitioner, or other health professional who has been specially trained and can provide this. They are likely to have access to much more expensive and sensitive equipment, and so this has its benefits.

In a biofeedback device or monitor, one way of giving feedback is by measuring your 'galvanic skin response' (GSR) or, in other words, how well your skin conducts electricity. The GSR can be used to measure stress or tension, because it increases as we become more tense, since we sweat more, and decreases as we relax. So a simple sensor attached to the fingers can be used to measure how well our skin is conducting electricity, and this can be displayed by a pointer, or converted to an audible tone, whose frequency or pitch rises and falls with the changing GSR. As we relax, this tone will fall gradually or even disappear altogether, giving us immediate feedback that our efforts to relax are working, and encouraging us to continue. This can be very effective, and many people enjoy this method of learning to relax. Another simple measure is skin temperature – the familiar stress dot or card is usually based on this kind of feedback. The principle underlying all this is the same as is used in the lie detector. Other monitors work similarly, but can monitor one or more of these: heart rate, temperature, respiration, muscle tension, blood pressure or brainwave activity.

Biofeedback can be remarkably effective, and many people enjoy this method of learning to relax. It doesn't really require any effort on your part, it just seems to happen. It's best not to analyse what's happening, but just to let it happen and go with the flow. I have found it appeals particularly to men, but many women find it incredibly useful too.

TAKING CARE WITH BIOFEEDBACK

Biofeedback is generally considered safe. However, it should generally not be used if you have depression, psychosis or another major mental health disorder. Biofeedback can potentially interfere with some medications, such as insulin, so patients with diabetes should exercise extra caution. Talk to your doctor to see whether biofeedback therapy is an appropriate treatment for you.

WHAT YOU CAN EXPECT FROM A THERAPIST

- ▶ *A typical biofeedback session lasts 30–60 minutes.*
- ▶ *The length and number of sessions will be determined by your condition and how quickly you learn to control your physical responses.*

- During a biofeedback session, a therapist will apply electrical sensors to different parts of your body, very similar to those used to produce an electrocardiograph (ECG).
- These sensors will monitor your body's physiological response to stress, and then feed the information back to you via cues such as a beeping sound or a flashing light, allowing you to begin to alter these by relaxing. The therapist will assist with this process, if needed.
- Your eventual goal will be to become so used to doing this, that you can produce these relaxation responses on your own, outside the therapist's office and without the help of technology.

Insight

Always, always, check that any therapist you use is adequately trained and insured, and belongs to an appropriate professional body. Don't be too embarrassed to check. Any good therapist won't mind your asking about this, and should have their certification easily to hand, to show you.

Alexander Technique

The Alexander Technique is a method which can help you perform all your usual activities without unnecessary tension. It can be applied to sitting, standing, walking, lifting, speaking – to whatever you do during your day.

Frederick Matthias Alexander (1869–1955) was an actor who developed chronic laryngitis while performing. He was determined to solve this problem, and his innovative answer to this was to carefully watch himself while speaking. What he noticed was that muscular tension in his neck appeared to be the cause of his vocal problem. He thought about this, and eventually decided that if tension in the neck was reduced, the head no longer compressed the spine and the spine was free to lengthen. He found that this worked. The Alexander Technique (AT), which bears his name, is a method of releasing unwanted muscular tension throughout the body.

As children, our posture and ease of movement are a joy to watch, but as we start to tense our muscles in reaction to many of life's worries and concerns, our posture deteriorates and produces unnecessary tension, which can become a lifelong habit, even producing pain in affected muscles. The Alexander Technique can help us to become aware of balance, posture and co-ordination while performing everyday actions. This brings into consciousness tensions throughout our body that have previously gone unnoticed, and it is these tensions which are very often the root cause of many common ailments. You can see this in action every day in other people. It is easy to see good examples of relaxed posture, and good balance and co-ordination, but bad examples are easily spotted too, where neck and shoulder tension are affecting every movement.

The AT teaches how to release unnecessary muscle tension. As most of this tension has built up very gradually over a number of years, you are unlikely to be aware that it is even there at all. New ways of moving while carrying out everyday actions which cause far less strain on the body are learned, and you can find out ways of sitting, standing and walking that put less strain on the bones, joints and muscles.

AT is intended to be learned with the help of a trained teacher, who uses a hands-on approach to guide you to the postural changes needed to effect a reduction in tension. Contact information for this is given in the 'Taking it further' section at the end of the book. In the meantime, here is some basic self-help you can try.

Try this – Self-AT

1   *Begin looking at yourself in a full-length, upright mirror. Notice in particular the relationship of your whole head to the rest of your body. Notice how this relationship changes as you perform simple activities like standing, talking, sitting, walking, lifting or holding something.*

2 Try changing how your head and body are positioned relative
   to each other, perhaps tilting your head a little forwards or
   backwards from the top of your neck and see if these small
   changes make any difference to how you are moving or
   standing, or to your breathing.
3 Alexander found that the most useful change he could make
   was to mentally direct his neck to be free of tension so that
   his head would balance lightly at the top of the spine.
   Try this. Does anything look or feel different?
4 Now, try doing the opposite. Stiffen your neck a little. What
   effect does this have on the position of your head, and your
   ability to breathe, speak and perform simple activities?

Insight

It's easy to feel that either you don't have the time, or you
shouldn't spend time on yourself using any of the ACTs
described here. But this is time well spent, and not wasted.
Remind yourself that we all need and deserve 'me-time', and
think of all the benefits you'll gain.

Reiki

The name reiki derives from the Japanese pronunciation of two
Chinese characters that are said to describe the energy itself: 'rei'
(meaning 'spirit', 'soul' or 'ghost') and 'ki' ('energy' or 'life force').
Reiki is a technique for stress reduction and relaxation that also
promotes healing. It is administered by touch, and is based on
the idea that an unseen 'life force energy' flows through us and is
what causes us to be alive. If our 'life force energy' is low, then we
are more likely to get sick or feel stress, and if it is high, we are
more capable of being relaxed, happy and healthy. Reiki energy is
channelled through the practitioner, directly into the client.

The ability to use reiki is not taught in the usual sense, but is
transferred to the student during a reiki class, given by a reiki

master, and this allows the student to tap into an unlimited supply of 'life force energy' to improve health and enhance the quality of life. Its use is not dependent on one's intellectual capacity or spiritual development and therefore is available to everyone. While reiki is spiritual in nature, it is not a religion. As in other therapies, there is nothing you must believe in to benefit from it.

If you decide to try reiki, you can take a first course, which includes using reiki on yourself. If you decide to contact a therapist, you will find that very few advertise their services in the conventional way, such as in telephone directories. Reiki practitioners work in various places, such as health and fitness centres, complementary health centres or from home, and often rely completely on word of mouth from their regular clients to contact others.

A REIKI SESSION

▶ *Allow about an hour for your session.*
▶ *It is best to wear loose-fitting garments, made of natural fabrics like wool or cotton. You are likely to be asked to remove any rings, watches or earrings prior to the session, so consider leaving these items at home.*
▶ *You will be asked to lie down on a massage table, couch or bed.*
▶ *All clothing is kept on, except for shoes.*
▶ *You may also be asked to remove or loosen your belt so that your breathing is not restricted in any way.*
▶ *Reiki practitioners will often create a relaxing atmosphere for their reiki sessions, setting the mood with the use of dimmed lights, meditative music, or bubbling water fountains. Some practitioners prefer to be in a place that is completely silent, without the distraction of music of any kind, to conduct their reiki sessions.*
▶ *The reiki practitioner will place their hands lightly on different parts of your body. Some practitioners will follow a predetermined sequence of hand placements, allowing their hands to rest on each body placement for between two and five minutes before moving on to the next.*

- *Empathic practitioners will freely move their hands in no particular order to the areas where they 'feel' reiki is most needed.*
- *Some reiki practitioners do not touch their clients. They will hover their palms a few inches above the body.*
- *Described as feeling warm, soothing and 'tingly', a recipient of reiki will often feel measurable heat emanating from the practitioner's hands.*
- *Once the reiki session is at an end, most therapists will discuss how things went, and any significant experiences or feelings either of you have had during the session.*
- *At the end of a session, most people feel relaxed and refreshed.*

Insight

Mixing with calm and laid-back people, and avoiding the flustered and driven, is a good way to keep your tension levels down.

Emotional Freedom Technique

The Emotional Freedom Technique (EFT) is a group of very simple processes which aim to help people achieve freedom from emotions that have created problems in their lives. The founder of EFT is Gary Craig, a Stanford engineering graduate and an ordained minister. Since its development in 1995, it has become very popular, and has been used to help people to cope with stress, anxiety, phobias, and for general confidence building.

> **Emotional Freedom Technique (EFT) is an emotional version of acupuncture, except needles aren't necessary.**
>
> Gary Craig, founder of EFT

Formal research evidence on the effectiveness of EFT is not yet available, but it is included here because it is an enormously popular technique, with strong anecdotal support. You can also easily try this for yourself – Gary provides all the information you need on his website. There are also training courses available, or you can see an EFT therapist, if you prefer.

The key process is to stimulate energy meridian points on your body by tapping on them with your fingertips. These points are to be found on the face, the hands, the head and the upper torso. Once learned, or shown to you, the process is easily remembered and can be done anywhere.

Humour and smiling

According to the International Stress Management Association, smiling is the first line of defence against tension and stress. When you smile your body releases feel-good hormones, while the stress hormone, cortisol, is reduced. Smiling helps you feel calm and in control. It lowers your blood pressure and makes you feel good about yourself. And laughter reduces the level of stress hormones and increases the level of health-enhancing hormones like endorphins, and neurotransmitters. Are you having a laugh?

Studies show that our response to stressful events depends on whether we view something as a 'threat' or a 'challenge'. Humour can give us a more light-hearted perspective and help us view events as 'challenges', thereby making them less threatening and more positive.

Research, evidence and statistics

▶ *A recent study showed that pre-school-aged children laugh up to 400 times a day, but by the time we reach adulthood, we laugh a mere 17 times per day on average!*
▶ *Britain is less happy than in the 1950s – despite the fact that we are three times richer. The proportion of people*

saying they are 'very happy' has fallen from 52 per cent in 1957 to just 36 per cent today. (Opinion poll for The Happiness Formula *series on BBC Two, presented by Mark Easton, 2006.)*

▶ *Research into happiness suggests that our levels of happiness change throughout our lives. People were asked how satisfied they are with their lives. Most people start off happy and become progressively less happy as they grow older. For many people, the most miserable period in their life is their 40s. After that most people's levels of happiness climb. (Andrew Oswald, Department of Economics, University of Warwick and Nattavudh Powdthavee, Institute of Education, University of London.)*

▶ *Dr Lee Berk and fellow researcher Dr Stanley Tan of Loma Linda University in California have been studying the effects of laughter on the immune system. To date their published studies have shown that laughing reduces stress hormones, and boosts immune function by raising levels of infection-fighting 'T-cells', disease-fighting proteins called Gamma-interferon, and B-cells, which produce disease-destroying antibodies. In addition, dopamine levels were also decreased. Dopamine is involved in the 'fight or flight response' and is associated with elevated blood pressure. Laughter also triggers the release of endorphins, the body's natural painkillers, and produces a general sense of relaxation and well-being.*

Happiness is indeed a hot topic these days, especially with 'positive' psychology an up-and-coming competitor to the more traditional type, which tries to fix the damage after it's done. It's more about prevention, and the promotion of a healthy and happy mind.

Laughter increases the number of antibody-producing cells, producing a stronger immune system, and reducing the physical effects of stress. It also gives a physical and emotional release, which can reduce all sorts of tension, and promote relaxation. A good laugh exercises the diaphragm, contracts the abdominal muscles (the abs) and even works the shoulders, leaving muscles more relaxed afterwards. A belly laugh results in muscle relaxation. This happens in two stages. While you laugh, the muscles that do not participate in the laugh relax. After you finish laughing, those muscles involved in the laughter start to relax.

Just using the muscles which make you smile, even in a 'put-on' rather than a genuine smile, starts to release endorphins. Laughter also takes your mind away from more negative thoughts and emotions. It is also very infectious. That is, if you are happy and laughing more often, this lifts the mood of those around you, making you someone others like to be around. Having friends and acquaintances who seek you out because they enjoy your company has immeasurable benefits.

> *The best way to cheer yourself up is to cheer someone else up.*
>
> Mark Twain, American writer, 1835–1910

You can bring humour and laughter into your life very easily. Go with your personal preferences, as humour is very individual – watch really funny television programmes or a comedy DVD. There's everything from comedy classic films, to funny clips, to sport's most amusing moments, and an endless list of stand-up comedians. Accept invitations to go out with friends, as humour is usually a part of that. Read a funny book. Learn how to do slapstick. Splash about in the pool with the children. Have a party for your birthday, or just for fun. All of these encourage a positive and cheerful atmosphere.

And of course, the simplest of all, smile more! Smile to yourself, smile at yourself, smile at other people. Learn to see the funny side of situations. Listen closely to those friends who are good at telling funny stories from their everyday life. How do they do it? Work it out and copy it. The effects of this can be dramatic. And even if you don't feel like it, you can still put on a smile. Research shows that the same beneficial effects happen even if you don't 'feel' the smile. These effects are activated by the muscles used to smile. This will encourage more and more completely natural smiles to come, and with them, more relaxation.

KEY POINTS

Look back over this chapter and choose the FOUR pieces of
information you found to be most interesting or helpful.
Write these here, or go back and underline or highlight them
in some way.

1 ....

2 ....

3 ....

4 ....

Look back over this chapter and choose the FOUR practical
suggestions you found to be most useful. Write these here, or go
back and underline or highlight them in some way.

1 ....

2 ....

3 ....

4 ....

Which TWO techniques or suggestions from this chapter would
you like to try out straight away?

Write these here, or go back and underline or highlight them in
some way.

1 ....

2 ....

Which TWO techniques or suggestions from this chapter would you like to work towards using regularly?

Write these here, or go back and underline or highlight them in some way.

1 ....

2 ....

10

Making the most of the Internet and modern technology

In this chapter you will learn:

- *in a very user-friendly way, with no assumed knowledge*
- *about different types of biofeedback*
- *about non-computerized devices which can aid relaxation*
- *how you can use a computer, software and the Internet to help you to relax.*

This chapter will cover how the Internet, computer software and other technology can be used to assist with the relaxation process. All of this is complementary material to dip into for those who are interested and comfortable with these media areas. So, it's up to you if you skip to the next chapter. That said, this material is no more difficult than any other part of the book, with no assumed knowledge, so this may be a chance to dip a toe in the water, and try out something new, if this is unknown territory. Everything will be explained here. There's nothing complicated or difficult.

There is so much already on offer in this field, and it is only going to expand. A vast range of material, resources, support and companionship are available easily and free of charge from the Internet. If you want to spend a few pounds, you can have even more hi-tech ways of relaxing literally at your fingertips, on screen, in your own home. If you have a little more to spend, the choice and variety expands still more. There are also numerous types of instruments or monitors which can be used to learn to relax, which have nothing to do with computers. So there's something for everyone.

If you are already at ease with computers and the Internet, you can skip the next section, which is for absolute beginners, and go straight to 'Contact information' on page 186.

For beginners

To get started, all you need is a desktop personal computer with access to the Internet. Computers come set up with this, so that's easy. You can also use a laptop computer or Apple Mac, but I won't cover these in detail here, as the controls and presentation are slightly different. The instructions provided should fill in any gaps for you.

All you need to do then is switch on. The first screen that appears after you switch on and the computer has finished loading itself up is called your 'desktop'. You know the computer is ready to use when the little hourglass which appears on screen while it is loading up changes to a stationary arrow in the centre of this first screen. On this 'desktop', just like a real desk, there will be a number of options for you to use. These are displayed on the screen as small symbols, or 'icons', about one centimetre high, with a name underneath telling you what they are.

TRY BEFORE YOU BUY

If you don't want to go to the expense of buying a computer, ask a friend if you can have a shot on theirs. Or, there are lots of 'Internet cafés' around, where you can have a coffee or a drink and hire the use of a computer with Internet access for an hour, or more if you wish. Local libraries and resource centres often have the same service available, possibly free. All of these have the advantage of having someone around to advise if you get stuck.

CONTACT INFORMATION

Though this chapter will be discussing the Internet, and the various websites and software available, this will be in general terms only, with more specific contact details and recommended sites given in the 'Taking it further' section at the end of this book. This kind of information changes almost by the second, so don't be put off if you have any difficulties accessing some of these sites, or finding what you are looking for. Simply use your 'Search' facility to track down what you are trying to find.

Think before you click

While the Internet is a wonderful resource with countless uses, you have to be careful with it, just like you would with any other medium. Here are some useful tips to follow:

▶ *Never give your financial information to anyone you cannot trust completely.*
▶ *Never give personal information to anyone you cannot trust completely.*
▶ *Only use reputable sites you are completely sure of.*
▶ *Make sure you are using a reputable and secure site if giving card details.*
▶ *Close down all windows that include personal or financial information, or password details, before leaving the computer – especially if using an Internet café, library or shared computer.*
▶ *Make sure you have anti-virus software installed.*
▶ *Make sure your anti-virus software is up to date – new viruses and other threats appear every day.*
▶ *If in doubt – don't.*

Non-computer-based equipment

But before talking about the Internet, there are many ways of using current technology without using a computer or accessing the net.

MAKE YOUR OWN RELAXING AUDIO OR VISUAL MATERIAL

If you have an iPod or MP3 player, or a combined MP3/mobile phone or similar, you can record and play any relaxing audio material you have, or make your own recording of whatever you find relaxing. This might be your own voice with particularly helpful or encouraging thoughts or material, or you can talk yourself through a relaxation technique. Or, perhaps there's someone else's voice with comments or ideas which you find calming or comforting. Then there may be certain sounds which you find relaxing, such as your garden, or a local beach, and so on.

Most mobile phones and digital cameras will also easily record a short video, with sound. So again, anything or anyone which can help you to relax can be stored in these recordings, and used when needed. The only limit is your imagination. It's so easy to make recordings these days.

BIOFEEDBACK DEVICES WITHOUT A COMPUTER

We have already mentioned the simplest of these in Chapter 9, when stress dots and cards, temperature sensors and basic biofeedback monitors were discussed. There are many more technically advanced biofeedback monitors available. Most simply require a couple of sensors to be attached using Velcro or other fixative. Alternatively, you simply need to place your fingers onto contacts. Devices are available right across the price range.

For tension in the scalp, face and neck muscles, a biofeedback headset is available which measures these contractions and instantly converts the signal into a pleasant tone where the pitch is proportional to the level of muscle tension. With the variations in the tone as a guide, you can quickly train your muscles to relax, relieving the discomfort and preventing future problems related to tense facial muscles, such as tension headaches.

There are many small devices, which can be worn on the wrist or on a finger, measuring pulse rate or blood pressure, both of which rise with stress. These are also used by athletes to ensure they are working out effectively. Many come in the form of a watch. A 'stress monitoring ring' can be worn which has a ten-colour temperature scale as part of its design. More devices are continually being developed.

Biofeedback using a computer is already a highly developed and readily available process, and will be discussed later in this chapter.

LIGHT AND SOUND GLASSES

Devices in the form of a headset, made up of a pair of special glasses and a set of headphones, are now available. They start at around £100, and are designed to create relaxation or other mood-changing effects through the use of sound and light stimulation. These are microprocessor-controlled devices. You simply select what you want from a list of options, put on headphones and glasses, and sit back and enjoy the experience, which can be for relaxation, stimulation, meditation or just plain fun depending on the session. Light and sound machines like these are very easy to use.

Insight

I've heard very good reports about light and sound glasses from people who have a pair. Not everyone's thing, but a real boon for some.

HANDHELD 'BRAIN-TRAINING' GAMES

These are a recent innovation, and the market is already growing fast. Keeping your brain active is the main focus, working on areas such as improving mathematical skills, memory and concentration, and encouraging left/right brain activity. This market is likely to move into other areas, including relaxation, so keep a look out.

Insight

It's not just 'brain-training' games, whether on or off the computer, which can help keep your brain 'fit'. Reflective activities like day-dreaming, telling stories and anecdotes to others, discussing ideas and issues, going to see a play, and reminiscing – will all do it too.

Podcasts on the Internet

New ways of communicating using the Internet and your computer are developing rapidly. There are 'podcasts' and the whole burgeoning field of downloading audio and video material onto your iPod or your MP3 or MP4 player, and all the rest.

It's all about being able to access sounds, pictures and video (sometimes called 'vidcasts' or 'video podcasts') on the net, and downloading them onto your computer, and then onto whichever equipment you have available. You may have an iPod or MP3 player that will take audio downloads, and an MP4 player for video material. MP3 players and iPods all play audio files, they are just made by different manufacturers. Then of course there is that new phenomenon, the 'podcast'.

You can think of a podcast as a radio show. Each show consists of a series of individual episodes that you can listen to in the manner of your choosing – on your PC, using your MP3 player, or on your iPod. You name the topic and you'll find podcasts about it. Not only do you have incredible choice, you can listen whenever and wherever you want.

There is so much material which you can download as audio (MP3) or video (MP4) files on the subject of relaxation, tension, stress and related topics, most of it of high quality, and much of it free. You can also find even more material for a small cost, and more still at higher cost. A plethora of relaxing, interesting and free screensavers or pictures for your desktop are available all over the net.

Most popular and well-known websites have podcasts as part of their resources. There are also 'podcast directories', which are websites devoted entirely to podcasts. Here are some of the most popular, covering every subject you can think of from relaxation to meditation and from yoga to reiki:

▶ *Podcast.net*
▶ *Odeo*
▶ *Podcast Pickle*
▶ *Podnova.*

If you want to listen to a podcast it's easy. Just download the 'episode' to your computer. You can then listen to it on your computer, or use your music software to transfer it to your MP3 player.

FREEBIES

Here is just a tiny selection of what you can find free – relaxing words, sounds, pictures and video – if you have a crawl around the web today. Tomorrow, who knows?

▶ *Free relaxing audio teamed with wonderful ever-changing related pictures. Examples range from rainforest sounds and birdsong, through to a purring cat, roaring ocean, sensational waterfalls, crackling log fire, whale sounds, a train on a track, as well as an old-fashioned typewriter, with or without carriage returns. There is even the sound of a vacuum cleaner, for those with a baby who can only sleep when the vacuum is on!*
▶ *Free calming screensavers and relaxing pictures for your desktop.*
▶ *Beautiful sunsets, lakes, flowers, mountain scenes.*

- *Plants, animals, landscapes, particular countries in the world, or parts of the UK, night scenes, day scenes.*
- *Audio downloads on health and fitness, time management, relaxation, meditation, mental health, and spirituality.*
- *Also thousands of links to free audio and video downloads relating to numerous famous authors as diverse as H. G. Wells, Mark Twain, Douglas Adams, Deepak Chopra and the Dalai Lama.*

Insight

All of this is great. I thoroughly enjoy today's hi-tech world and all it has to offer. But I try not to forget there's a real world out there too, and I need to be a part of that as well. It's all about balance.

Biofeedback using a computer

In my 20 and more years involved in stress and relaxation, the subject which has interested most people, and on which I've been asked many questions, is *biofeedback*. With a dual background in physics and in psychology, this is a subject dear to my heart!

When I first used a simple biofeedback monitor in 1982, it cost me £9.99 from a national electrical chain, and there was a kit form available which you could make up yourself if you were handy with a soldering iron! I remember being surprised that the kit was more expensive than the made-up version – I've never quite understood that. There were very few computers around then, and certainly no Internet, so finding out more about biofeedback wasn't easy.

But now it's child's play for those of you who might be interested in learning more about it, or finding out something about it for the first time. There is an abundance of websites out there, all bursting at the seams with information on all kinds of biofeedback, and offering devices to suit all pockets and applications.

As we discussed in Chapter 9, biofeedback, as its name would suggest, involves giving some form of immediate feedback to a person, as to whether they are relaxing or not, based on a biological or physiological measure. For example, this can be feedback on brain, muscle or skin activity, or on breathing rate or blood pressure. So, as we relax we receive immediate feedback of some kind to show that our efforts to relax are working, and this encourages us to continue.

In the case of many simple devices, feedback on 'galvanic skin response' (GSR – how well your skin conducts electricity) is used to measure stress. This increases as we become more stressed, since we sweat more, and decreases as we relax. Another simple measure is skin temperature, which decreases with stress, as blood supply to the peripheries is reduced, and increases as we relax – the familiar stress dot or card is usually based on this kind of feedback.

Biofeedback can be remarkably effective, and many people enjoy this method of learning to relax. There are many websites devoted to biofeedback, offering in-depth explanations about it, and giving current research findings, and practical advice about different types of biofeedback and how to use them. Many offer a free 'e-zene', or e-mailed magazine, at regular intervals, or organize workshops and tasters.

An interesting and exciting variety of software is also now available, and is growing and developing all the time. These allow you to learn and practise advanced biofeedback techniques as you are entranced by breathtaking three-dimensional landscapes, soothing music and inspiring visuals, or as you play specially devised games. Your physiological responses are measured using a simple monitor, which comes with the software, and this information is fed directly into the computer. Most come with their own training manual with tips and strategies for meditation, searching for precious stones that will heal and restore inner peace, playing mental games or solving puzzles, landing aircraft, and all of that kind of thing. You can then look at graphs and summaries of how your body has been responding throughout, all compiled effortlessly, and stored for future reference on the computer.

Insight

Using this kind of software either really appeals or is a real switch off. I wonder which of these groups you'll fall into?

Social networking sites

One of the important aspects of being able to relax and be at ease with yourself is having good social support. Preferably this would be in the flesh, so to speak, but a useful add-on these days can be the social networking site (SNS). Even in the world of business, networking sites are becoming a crucial part of meeting and keeping new clients, and keeping in touch with colleagues. Many people now have their favourite site as their home page on their computer, checking it every day for what's new and who's doing what. And of course, many people use it to add their bit about their life and goings on, be these exciting and stimulating or, more likely, mundane and everyday. We now glory in the world of the trivial. And there's nothing wrong with that. It makes a change from all the major stresses we face every day in our macro world.

You're probably all familiar with the first well-known SNS which came into being in 2000, Friends Reunited, a site where old school friends can make contact again, should they want to do this. This site has now diversified into reuniting university students, old workmates, sports teams, and even old neighbours. It has had its controversies, but it currently has some 19 million members. However, in that short time, the whole idea of SNSs has developed incredibly, with hundreds of sites now catering for any kind of networking, and providing for all sorts of mutual interests in this global village we call planet Earth.

HOW TO JOIN AN SNS

1 *First register with your chosen site. You can usually have a site tour without registering, so you can have a look over what's on offer, to help you decide if you want to get on board or not.*
2 *Then, fill out your profile with your photo and interests, your work and education history, recent news and activities, and so on. You can also post videos, articles and other relevant items. You can read the messages your friends leave for you, and you can see photos which have been left for you from around the site. You can also share your thoughts by writing notes or importing your 'blog' (see page 195).*
3 *Most SNSs are made up of many networks, each based around a company, region or school. Join the networks that reflect your real-life communities to learn more about the people who work, live or study around you.*
4 *People can only see the profiles of confirmed friends and the people in their networks.*
5 *When you log in, you'll see all the latest news and activity from your friends. And you can check out photos and notes your friends have added, and see what groups they've joined or created.*
6 *You can also see which of your friends have upcoming birthdays, and check out the videos, articles, links and other items your friends are sharing with you.*

PRIVACY AND SECURITY

SNSs usually have specific privacy settings for photos, notes, each part of your profile and so forth. You can block individuals you don't want knowing you exist on the particular SNS, and you can create a 'limited profile' to hide certain parts of your profile from specific friends.

An important word of caution: These sites do have drawbacks, which you may well have heard about more than about the sites themselves. Identity theft is always a risk when you give information about yourself. Perhaps worse, depending how you look at it, is people masquerading as someone they are not, in order to exploit you in some way. This can be especially nasty on the sites used by young people. So be careful, only use well-known sites, and keep your wits about you. Never risk anything you aren't 100 per cent sure about.

POPULAR SITES

Two of the most popular SNSs are **Facebook** (400 million) and **MySpace** (130 million). It's difficult even to comprehend those kinds of numbers, and the huge amount of networking going on in this way.

Here is a selection of other specialist sites, some big and some small, which anyone can join:

Site	Interests of members	Number of members
LinkedIn	Business – must be introduced by an existing member.	65 million
Friendster	General	90 million
Geni.com	Families, genealogy	15 million
Hi5	General	80 million
Windows Live Spaces	Blogging	120 million
Reunion.com	Locating friends and family. Keeping in touch.	28 million
Twitter	General	75 million

Blogs and blogrolls

If you want to be part of the technological twenty-first century, you really can't afford to miss out on blogging. And of course, relaxation and stress-related issues of all kinds will be a part of today's blogging, just as every other subject will be.

In the world of blogs, or the 'blogosphere', as it is known, you will find up-to-the-minute chat, news, experiences, information and press releases on any and every subject. Blogging has also been described as a very cathartic activity, and so can help individuals to relax, and to combat stress itself. You can pour everything out into your own daily or weekly blog, safely releasing all the pent-up pressure and tension and the frustration of living.

There are also 'blog rings', which are linked communities of bloggers who have a shared interest. So any stress-related topic should be covered and community support offered. These rings can be found via Technorati's blog finder (see 'Taking it further' at the end of the book). If you can't find exactly what you are looking for, you can even establish a blog ring for yourself.

SO WHAT EXACTLY IS 'BLOGGING'?

It is widely accepted that Jorn Barger coined the term 'weblog' in 1997, by combining the words 'website' and 'logging', as he was logging his own comments and choice of links to news and information sites on his own website. 'Weblog' was then historically shortened to 'blog' by Peter Merholz in 1999. Blogging has developed and grown extraordinarily quickly, and it is reckoned that 100,000 new blogs come into being every day, to join the millions already there. The 'blogosphere' is thought to double every five months. Just when we thought the Internet had given up all of its greatest surprises and innovations.

In a very short time blogging has grown from one individual's idiosyncratic use of his own website, to become a new channel for distributing news and other information, whether written, or in picture, audio or video form, extremely rapidly, all over the world. So opinions, pictures, information and recommendations of all kinds can span the globe unbelievably quickly, thanks to the fast and easy specific programming and software which has been developing alongside this remarkable innovation on the web.

Insight

Blogging and looking at other people's blogs has become a way of life for lots of people. It's a great way to keep in touch with what everyone else is doing, and to keep a record of your life and experiences.

Rather than using a popular search engine like Yahoo or Google, you may find that using more specific searches is more effective to find suitable sites. You can use blog-specific search sites, or use blog portals or directories. When I keyed in 'stress management' in one such site, 13,000 results were produced, including one blog posted just 12 minutes previously, and another one seven minutes before that, which had already been viewed by 70 people! I was also provided with a day-by-day graph of the number of blogs containing 'managing stress' posted in the past month.

Here are just a few of the most popular sites you might like to start your blogging journey from:

▶ *Technorati*
▶ *Blogger*
▶ *Blog Catalog*
▶ *WordPress*
▶ *Global Voices Online.*

The biggest and best blogs in the blogosphere are measured by the number of people who have made them a 'favourite'. Every good blog also includes a list of the author's own favourite blogs – called, what else... the 'blogroll'. The most visited blogs can be tracked down via the website popularity index, Popdex.

All this means that, unlike most topics covered in the book so far, this is one which you can get actively involved in creating, if you want. You can get your thoughts and views or experiences of relaxation and stress out there easily and quickly. And if you want to, you can contribute to, and even influence or lead public opinion in your own small corner, or over the entire planet. You can even become the world's newest guru on relaxation, if you want.

KEY POINTS

Look back over this chapter and choose the FOUR pieces of information you found to be most interesting or helpful. Write these here, or go back and underline or highlight them in some way.

1 ....

2 ....

3 ....

4 ....

Look back over this chapter and choose the TWO practical suggestions you found to be most useful. Write these here, or go back and underline or highlight them in some way.

1 ....

2 ....

Which THREE techniques or suggestions from this chapter would you like to try out straight away?

Write these here, or go back and underline or highlight them in some way.

1 ....

2 ....

3 ....

Which TWO techniques or suggestions from this chapter would you like to work towards using regularly?

Write these here, or go back and underline or highlight them in some way.

1 ....

2 ....

11

Relaxation and your feelings

In this chapter you will learn:
* *how relaxation can help with anger or jealousy*
* *ways that relaxation helps you deal better with criticism*
* *about anxiety, phobias and OCD.*

A huge variety of ways of relaxing have now been described, giving the opportunity to learn a range of skills for different situations, with many more still to try out, or use in the future. With these skills now available to you, this chapter and the following two will bring all that you've learned so far together, and see how to make maximum use of them in a range of specific situations.

In this chapter, the spotlight will be on how relaxation can help you to deal better with feelings such as anger or jealousy, and to cope with criticism and put-downs. All of these are potent sources of tension, and can create discord in relationships, in families, or at work. Ideas on how to cope better with different types of anxiety will also be presented.

A dual approach

Sometimes being able to relax isn't just about the direct approach of using a technique. It can also be about being more skilled and confident in dealing with a situation or a feeling, and about having a better understanding of what's happening to you. This chapter is very much about approaching relaxation from this more indirect angle, along with the more direct approach taken so far. A dual approach.

_____

Anger

As we grow up, all of us develop ways of thinking which are our own. Much of this is pre-programmed, but some of it comes from our experiences of life, and even from copying other people. We all have our own habits, and patterns of thought, which we use routinely, and don't really question. Most of us assume everybody thinks in the same way as we do – but this is not the way it works.

Try this – Analysing your anger

Do you ever have thoughts which include these words?

▶ *If it wasn't for you...*
▶ *You've ruined everything...*
▶ *You are never there for me...*
▶ *They have let me down again...*
▶ *I'm going to explode...*
▶ *They've made me look stupid...*
▶ *How dare he...*
▶ *I hate you...*
▶ *I hate this place...*
▶ *You are so selfish...*
▶ *Why don't you listen to me?*
▶ *He/She is so stupid...*
▶ *There you go disagreeing with me again...*

These are 'angry thoughts', and most people have some of these sometime. Do you have other 'angry thoughts'? Take your time. Really think about it and be honest with yourself. All of these thoughts can easily become thinking habits, which produce angry feelings. And these can go on to produce angry and aggressive behaviour, which is the real problem. Everyone can have an occasional burst of angry behaviour, and as long as this is rare, and doesn't do any harm, then it can be coped with. But if this is a frequent occurrence, and is interfering with a person's life and relationships, then it's time to do something about it. Anger and angry behaviour are habits, and you can change a habit with some effort, some understanding, and some know-how.

> *When anger rises, think of the consequences.*
>
> Confucius, Chinese philosopher (551–479 BC)

SOME UNHELPFUL BELIEFS ABOUT ANGER

Most people think that being prone to anger is part of your make-up. Something you were born with. Inherited from your father, perhaps, or your mother, or Uncle George. Yes, we may inherit a tendency to be more *emotional* – and that is not necessarily a bad thing – it probably means you can be a sensitive and caring person. But how we react to and deal with that emotion is something we *learn*. So, as such, it is not fixed, and can be changed. So, yes, you may react with emotion to being under threat, criticized unfairly or frustrated, but it's what you do next that matters. You don't have to deal with that situation by becoming angry. There are always choices in how to deal with any situation.

People can also believe that if anger isn't released, some damage will occur, or that they'll explode – something like a pressure cooker. Again, this is not so. Just as you can switch off the gas on a pressure cooker, you can switch off the gas on your anger too, with no harm done. Of course preventing it building up in the first place is the best strategy, because feeling angry itself does increase heart rate and blood pressure, and this can be harmful if repeated frequently.

Try this – When you feel the rage rising...

If you can, leave the room or situation:

▶ *Go for a brisk walk or run outside, until you can remember the good things of life.*

> ▶ *Release the energy constructively by doing something*
> *physically demanding and useful like gardening, aerobics,*
> *cleaning, whatever.*

ANGER IS A PROCESS

Anger doesn't just happen out of the blue. Nor does it happen because it's 'just the way you are', as mentioned previously. No, anger is the end result of a process. That is to say, it's not just something that erupts in you for no reason, and at any time. It may sometimes feel that way though, as if it just flashes up suddenly, and takes over.

Yes, anger is the end point of a process. And sometimes that's a long building process. But sometimes it's a process that can happen in the blink of an eye. It can, and it frequently does, take everyone by surprise.

But the useful thing about a process is that, however quickly it may happen, it is made up of steps, and so we can intervene somewhere along the way in those steps, to prevent that anger rising in the first place. And, we can reverse that process. We can stop the end product, anger, being produced at all.

Insight

Many people who are having problems with anger are not aware that there has been a build up to it. To them, it feels just like lightning, suddenly striking out of the blue, totally beyond their control. Understanding this process and build-up is the key to regaining control over anger.

The build-up

Being a process also means that your anger can build up over a very long period, simmering away quietly in the background, for hours, days or even longer. This frustration can build and build, like a tap dripping inside of you, until it develops a head of steam and then, for no particular reason, it can suddenly explode from covert anger into overt anger.

Why does it happen? Anger is a natural human emotional response, part of the 'fight or flight' response which evolved millions of years ago to help us to deal with physical danger, such as the threat from wild animals. We still experience it today when we are in danger physically, as we've seen already. And we can also find ourselves in the 'fight or flight' situation if we feel in danger 'psychologically'. Some relevant examples of this response producing anger would be when there is danger to us 'as a person' because of:

▶ *a threat*
▶ *emotional hurt*
▶ *confrontation*
▶ *criticism*
▶ *violation*
▶ *put-downs*
▶ *humiliation*
▶ *frustration.*

Nowadays, anger outbursts can happen especially:

▶ *with your family or partner*
▶ *with the person or child you are carer for*
▶ *with colleagues at work*
▶ *with people you manage*
▶ *with your manager at work*
▶ *with people in authority*
▶ *on the road in the car*
▶ *in a queue anywhere*
▶ *with shop assistants*
▶ *on the telephone*
▶ *on the computer.*

So, the person who pushes ahead in the queue at the supermarket, the receptionist who won't give you an appointment when you want it, the employee who just can't get things right, the toddler who will not leave the TV remote control alone, a partner or parent criticizing you yet again, all of these can bring out the worst. And, the worst seems to come out more easily when there is some element of anonymity. It can be so much easier just to let rip in road rage, over the phone or in an e-mail.

Remember: Try not to use angry words, or angry actions. Instead, try to explain and talk about what your feelings are, and why.

Your triggers

Whether we react to situations with anger or not, and what we then do is very personal. We are all different. That's because this process has, in general, been learned as we grew up, or from our life experiences as adults. We learn by experience, and we learn by copying others around us. But there is no great benefit from analysing this too much. It's what you do from here on that matters. Working out your own triggers and patterns is what will help most.

Try this – Your angry feelings

Have a think about these questions. There are no 'right' answers. This is just a chance to think things through. Jot down your thoughts for each on a spare piece of paper or in a notebook. This is just for you, so keep these notes somewhere private if you'd rather nobody sees them. Use short notes, headings, lists, sentences, whatever suits you best.

1 *Think back to times you've become angry. Try to describe exactly how it made you feel at the time you were angry. Did you feel it:*
   ▷ *in your body?*
   ▷ *in your head?*
   ▷ *in your mind?*
2 *Again thinking back to times you've been angry, how did you feel afterwards, when the anger had gone?*
3 *What sorts of situations make you angry? What are the triggers?*

If someone becomes angry, there will always have been something that has set this off – a trigger, in other words. These triggers are not only to be found in people or events, but just as often they are in the angry person's own thoughts. Being aware of triggers is an essential part of coping with anger.

Try this – Discovering your triggers

Think carefully about when you have been angry. Note down your answers to these questions:

1 *Which things outside of you are your triggers (people, places, events)?*
2 *Which things inside of you are your triggers (worries, upsetting memories, emotions, other thoughts)?*

Coping with your anger

NEUTRAL THOUGHTS TO REPLACE ANGRY ONES

It can be helpful to generate alternatives to the 'angry thoughts'. These alternative, more 'neutral' thoughts should not produce anger. This takes a bit of practice, but you'll soon become much better at noticing and catching those 'angry thoughts' and working out alternative 'neutral thoughts'. This is really worth the effort, as it really can work. Here is an activity to help get this started.

Try this – Neutralize your thoughts

Over the next few days and weeks, look out for your triggers and the 'angry thoughts' they produce. In your notebook, write down the 'angry thought' as shown, along with the alternative 'neutral thought' you came up with. Here are a few to start you off. You need to practise this until it becomes a habit.

Angry thought	Alternative neutral thought
He always lets me down.	He makes mistakes sometimes, but most of the time he's great.
	He tries really hard, but he's very tired with the kids right now.
She is looking at me as if I'm stupid.	She is looking, but I don't know what she's thinking.
	She may be worrying about something.
	She may not have her contacts in.
He doesn't care about me.	He has let me down this time, but he is usually very loving, so he does care.
	Everybody has an off day. He does care really.

CHALLENGING 'ANGRY THOUGHTS'

Angry thoughts can also be approached in the same way as any other 'unhelpful' thoughts. That is by 'challenging' them by asking the following questions. This helps to diffuse the anger and encourage more relaxed thinking.

Try this – Questions to ask yourself when you are angry

1 *What is the evidence for this thought being true?*
  ▷ *Evidence supporting the idea.*
  ▷ *Evidence against the idea.*
2 *Is there an alternative explanation?*
3 *Is this worth getting angry about?*
4 *What would I tell a friend if they were in the same situation?*

RELAXATION TECHNIQUES

By now you should have some idea of which relaxation techniques
you prefer, and which work well for you in different situations.
Some long slow methods, some faster methods, some breathing
techniques, and so on. Deciding on an answer to the following
questions is important for dealing well with anger.

1 *Which method of relaxing works best for you when angry?*
2 *What about your breathing?*
3 *When is the best time to use relaxation?*
4 *Which calming image can you use to replace your angry
 thoughts?*

Now that you have a better understanding of anger, here is a
summary of suggestions for coping with anger, using the dual
approach of relaxation techniques and other specialist skills:

▶ *It is not people or events that make you angry, it is your
 reaction to them that makes you angry.*
▶ *Getting very angry is not good for you and is never helpful.*
▶ *Try not to use angry words – explain and talk about what
 your feelings are, and why.*
▶ *Use a relaxation technique to keep your voice relaxed and low
 key, without an 'edge' to it.*
▶ *Prevent highs and lows of your blood sugar by avoiding
 sugary food and eating small and healthy regular meals.*
▶ *Regular exercise will help you to even out mood swings,
 relieve tension and frustration, and make you feel happier too.*
▶ *Look out for your triggers, and immediately when you are
 aware of anger beginning, use a relaxation technique to 'nip it in
 the bud', counteract the feeling, and relax your tense muscles.*

- *Take time to think, find out more, and respond to people – don't jump straight in.*
- *Become aware of, challenge and question your angry thoughts.*
- *Replace angry thoughts with neutral, helpful thoughts.*
- *Replace angry thoughts with calming images, e.g. a beach, a quiet brook, your anger as a fire inside you being 'put out' by a bucket of water.*
- *Listen and communicate actively with others.*
- *Make sure to keep your posture relaxed and at ease.*
- *Neither stare at nor avoid the gaze of others.*
- *Don't try to mind-read other people's thoughts and intentions – you're usually wrong.*
- *Don't jump to conclusions.*
- *Be more assertive – learn how to accept criticism, deal with authority figures, and say 'no'.*
- *If need be, make an excuse and leave the situation for a minute or two, allow yourself time to calm down, and return when calmer.*
- *Always leave a situation and use relaxation to calm down if you feel you are going to be verbally or physically aggressive.*

Insight

I have been surprised over the years at the number of people who just never thought to excuse themselves and take a break to calm down when they were angry. But I suppose that's because anger clouds your judgement. You have to be ready to lift that cloud, if it should drift into your world.

Coping with someone else who is angry

I am not talking about a violent person here – that would belong in another book. No, what I'm thinking of here is aggressive, angry behaviour, which you don't feel is likely to escalate to violence. Of course, anger progressing to violence is always a possibility, and you should be prepared to opt out, and get out of the situation or summon help as quickly as possible if you feel violence is threatened. Never take risks with your safety.

Even though you may have a problem with being angry yourself, that doesn't make being faced with an angry person any easier. It is still frightening and disturbing. So, what can you do when faced with an angry person? One of the best ways to begin to understand how to deal with other angry people is to learn about anger. It is much easier then to understand what is happening when you come into contact with an angry person, and to know how best to react. So make sure you've read everything which has already been covered in this chapter. Here are some additional suggestions.

SOMEONE YOU KNOW WHO IS ANGRY

If a particular time of day or setting often produces an argument or anger in someone you know, avoid having discussions at that time. For example, last thing at night can be a problem time, or when someone has just come home from work and is tired and needs a break. Weekends and holidays can also be difficult times. It's common to raise issues in the car, when there is no escape. Choose another time to talk about things, when you are likely to be calmer.

It also helps if you can become aware of signs in the person that they are heading for a bout of anger. If you know the person, you can become aware of these if you look out for them. This might include:

- ▶ *nail-biting*
- ▶ *drinking more than usual*
- ▶ *eating more or less than usual*
- ▶ *smiling less than usual*
- ▶ *being less touchy-feely than usual*
- ▶ *being less intimate than usual*
- ▶ *going quieter than usual*
- ▶ *over-working*
- ▶ *speeding up at everything*
- ▶ *driving too fast*
- ▶ *breathing faster than usual*
- ▶ *appearing tense*
- ▶ *taking it out on the pet/s.*

SOMEONE YOU DON'T KNOW

Clearly, you can't be aware of these earlier first signs, so be alert in terms of their body language, general behaviour and thinking. We are quite good at reading people and knowing when a person is becoming angry. This is a basic survival mechanism. So trust your instincts on this, and take appropriate action as soon as you suspect there is a problem.

First things first
At this early stage, and all the way through an interaction with someone who is angry, use a relaxation technique to stay relaxed, but alert enough to think and act carefully.

Faced with an angry person, the main thing you want to be thinking about is using all your energy to protect your self-esteem and calm the situation. So you must get your thinking right. Here are some helpful thoughts for you to have in your mind at this stage:

▶ *I am not responsible for this person's feelings.*
▶ *I can improve things by keeping calm myself.*
▶ *An angry exchange rarely solves problems.*
▶ *Anger is temporary and it will pass.*
▶ *Angry people are often angry with themselves, not me.*
▶ *Angry people are often angry with someone else, not me.*
▶ *I can expect exaggeration from an angry person.*
▶ *I mustn't expect this person to think fairly just now.*
▶ *Angry people say things they don't mean.*

Body language and assertiveness
Respond in a way which does not inflame the situation. A relaxed body and especially a slow, warm and calm voice can make all the difference. A calming tone and quality of voice is one of your most important assets in this type of interaction. This will help you to stay calm, but it will also have the effect of calming the other person down.

So, you could use techniques such as:

- *asking for more information*
- *clarifying the situation*
- *checking your understanding*
- *accepting realistic criticism*
- *reflecting on what they are saying.*

It is always wise to make sure that the angry person is not between you and the door, just in case you need to leave. You could even say you need some air, and use that excuse to open a door or window, so that you can summon help easily by shouting, should that be necessary. Seldom required, but best to be prepared.

Use active listening skills
Anger is often caused by a person feeling that they are not being heard. So in a warm and calm voice you might say things like:

- *I hear what you are saying.*
- *I see that you are very unhappy with the service you've had.*
- *When would suit you better?*
- *You've certainly had a raw deal with that.*
- *I appreciate that you're not happy with my being late again.*

Avoid using phrases including 'I understand how you feel', as this often produces an angry response along the lines of, 'you can't possibly understand' or, 'nobody understands'. And don't be tempted to tell the person to relax or calm down, as this usually has the opposite effect. Remaining calm yourself is the best way to calm down an angry person.

Make an empathic statement
If the angry person sees that you know they are angry, this may defuse things for them. So you could say something like:

- *I can see you are very upset.*
- *You do seem angry about this.*
- *This has clearly distressed you.*

But you must use a warm and friendly tone in your voice for this – the whole tone changes if you add an edge of any kind to your voice. This is something you can practise if need be.

Be conciliatory

Showing a commonly understood gesture of conciliation can have an amazingly rapid effect in defusing a situation and the anger will disappear. So you could do any of these, again being careful with your tone of voice:

▶ *make a genuine apology*
▶ *make a statement of regret*
▶ *offer a reasonable and fair compromise*
▶ *acknowledge the other person's right to their view*
▶ *accept your share of responsibility for the problem.*

Leave analysing the problem till later

There's no point in trying to sort everything out while the person is angry. If there are loose ends, talk about them later, when you've both had time to calm down. Choose a good time and place for both of you. So use a phrase like: 'We don't seem to be getting anywhere with this just now. How about we meet again tomorrow to talk it through?'

Jealousy

> *Our envy of others devours us most of all.*
>
> Alexander Solzhenitsyn, Russian author (1918–2008)

Jealousy is another common feeling which causes enormous problems and heightens tension. It can happen to anyone, though some people seem to be more prone to it than others. There can be any sort of basis to it, be it in a relationship, or perhaps someone getting the job you wanted, or the house, or the car, or whatever. Like anger, the dual approach of increased understanding along with relaxation techniques and specialist skills can be helpful.

And like anger, jealousy is deeply based in thinking habits, and thinking triggers. Here are some tips:

▶ You *cause your jealousy, not the other person. The problem is in* your thinking, *not in their behaviour.*

▶ *Your imagination is probably far too good, and gets carried away with itself. Just because you think it, doesn't make it real.*

▶ *You don't have to express a feeling, just because you feel it. Keep your jealousy and jealous thoughts to yourself.*

▶ *The more you think your jealous thoughts, the bigger and more reasonable they may seem, but that doesn't make them any more true.*

▶ *Use distraction to chase away your jealous thoughts. Do something else, or think something else. Use relaxing words or images to replace the jealous ones.*

▶ *Use relaxation to calm and soothe your bruised nervous system.*

▶ *Challenge your jealous thoughts in the same way as you challenge angry or worrying thoughts – don't just believe them because they are in your head. Think about what evidence there is for and against your thoughts. What are the chances?*

JEALOUSY IN RELATIONSHIPS

The more jealous scenes you have, and the more you accuse, the more you will damage a relationship. This scenario can be repeated again and again in relationship after relationship. It's all about not being able to trust the other person. Why? There are so many reasons for this, most usually that you've been hurt before by trusting someone, or that you don't have sufficient faith in yourself as being worthy of another person caring for you, and remaining faithful to you.

Remember:

1 *Jealousy makes you behave in the opposite way to the way which encourages love.*

2 *Love is based on trust. So trust completely until you are proved wrong. If you can't trust yet, pretend until you can.*

3 *It takes time to be able to trust, and not to feel jealousy, but here are some other thoughts to remember which may help:*

▷ *Remember that you are a good person. Your partner wants to love you. That's why you have a relationship.*

▷ *You are a lovable person. Remember that always. You don't always need someone to tell you.*

▷ *Thinking a thought doesn't mean it will happen.*

▷ *We all have more than enough love to go round. Our capacity to love has no limits.*

Dealing with criticism and put-downs

Criticizing others has become something of a spectator sport, with reality TV using this for entertainment purposes. It's easy to be drawn into this, and see it as harmless fun. But it can be so different if we are the ones who are being criticized and put down. Some people can handle this without a backward glance, but for most people, it is an unwanted part of daily life, which brings with it tension and disquiet.

You will be familiar with my dual approach now, and handling criticism is best dealt with in this way too. Using relaxation to lessen the emotional response makes it much easier to use the specialist skills described here. That said, this does require a bit of practice, and that's definitely how to approach this. Try out the suggestions below in a situation which isn't too important, before gradually moving to more and more important situations, such as an appraisal at work, or your partner complaining about your tidiness at home.

HANDLING DIRECT CRITICISM

This can be one of the hardest things to cope with in an assertive way. It can bring back memories of being criticized by a parent or a teacher, and not being allowed to respond. But you aren't in that kind of powerless position now, so remind yourself that human beings are equal, and that you have self-worth and self-esteem, just like everyone else. Remind yourself of this if necessary until you build a positive self-image and feeling of worth which comes from inside you. This will of course take time, and you've only just made a start. In this way, you'll be responding on a more level playing field.

You may well have found yourself accepting unfair criticism and taking it to heart. This will only undermine your confidence and increase tension. So, the first thing to do is to learn the difference between criticism that is realistic and fair comment, and criticism that is unfair and unfounded. Here are some assertive ways to respond to both of these types of criticism.

I have learned more from my mistakes than from my successes.
Sir Humphry Davy, chemist and inventor of the Miners'
Safety Lamp, 1778–1829

Coping with fair criticism
We all make mistakes and mess up sometimes. It's just what people do. So there is no shame in this, and no need to let it upset you. Use a relaxation technique to help you deal with the emotional response. Then, there are two possible ways to react to fair criticism, both of which can remove its sting.

Try this – Realistic and fair comments

Accept them
The simplest response is to accept the criticism without expressing guilt or making an apology. We all make mistakes, and the best thing is to hold your hand up to it, correct the situation, and learn from it. It has been said that the person who never made a mistake never did anything.

'You didn't make a very good job of that.'

'No, I didn't did I? I'll have to have another go at it.'

OR

Ask for information
Another way of coping is to accept the criticism but ask
for more information about it from the person doing the
criticizing.

'You didn't clean the flat very well.'

'No, it wasn't too good, was it? Was it the hoovering, or was
it the bathroom that was the problem?'

HANDLING PUT-DOWNS

Sometimes people can be openly critical and insulting, and that
can be hard to cope with. But more often, they can engage in using
what are called 'put-downs'. This is a more manipulative and
veiled form of criticism. Sometimes people don't even realize that
they are doing it. You may even have done it yourself. You know
the kind of thing, like these examples:

1 *'I do like your new car. I was going to buy one just like it, but
   I thought it wouldn't suit my image.'*
2 *'You're looking good today. It's good to see you in something
   new.'*
3 *'Are you sure that's the best way to do that?'*
4 *'Haven't you finished that report yet?'*
5 *'If I were you, I'd have used the blue paint on that wall.'*

These kinds of comments are usually said with a smile, but they
leave you with a sour taste in your mouth, and a vague feeling
that you've been criticized, but you're not really sure. So you
don't quite know what to say. Or maybe you react aggressively
because you do feel instinctively that you're being attacked in
some way.

Put-downs like these can make you feel small and can dent your
identity and self-confidence, and make you feel tense and anxious.

They are particularly destructive in the long term, or in a close personal relationship. So how do you deal with them? Mainly by letting the person know that you are aware of what they've actually implied, but doing so in a relaxed and assertive way. Use your relaxation to calm yourself and deal with the tension the put-down has brought out in you.

Then, you can acknowledge the criticism and back this up with a positive comment as in the responses in 1, 2 and 3 below. As ever, use a calm, warm and friendly voice. Or, you can just 'fog' the issue, by vaguely acknowledging their implied criticism as in 4 and 5 below. 'Fogging' of this kind can be quite disarming.

So you might say, in response to the above put-downs:

1 *'Yes, I know it's quite a basic car, but I got an amazingly good deal on it.'*
2 *'Yes, I know that my wardrobe needs some improving, but I've had more important things to spend my money on recently.'*
3 *'Yes, I'm sure your way of doing it would have been useful, but Jerry asked me to do it this way today.'*
4 *'Yes, maybe it has taken me longer than usual to finish it.'*
5 *'Yes, the blue paint probably would have been better on this wall.'*

Once faced with what they are actually saying to you out in the open, most people will usually then back down, and won't try this on you again. People only do this to you if you let them.

Coping with unfair criticism

If criticism seems to be unfair, once again, use relaxation to help you to stay calm and in control, with a warm and relaxed voice. Your tone of voice makes all the difference here. Here are three possible ways to deal with things:

1 **Disagree with it** – *calmly and assertively disagree with the criticism.*

'You're always late for meetings.'
'No, I'm not always late. I may have been late once or twice, but I'm definitely not always late.'

2 **Ask for information** – *you can use this technique to accept the criticism, but also continue to ask for more information (as discussed on pages 216–17) until the criticizer wishes they hadn't raised the subject!*

3 **Use fogging** – *fog the issue, giving the criticizer nothing substantial to get a hold on. You can use phrases like:*
'Perhaps you are right...'
'Sometimes I can be...'
'You could be right...'
'There could be some truth in that...'
So the criticism seems to be accepted, but is actually having little impact. This will also put the criticizer off criticizing you unfairly again.

Giving criticism

Criticism can be given very badly, usually because the giver is uptight about it. So use relaxation to make sure you are calm and in control. Here are some other tips:

▶ *Make sure to praise the positive too, on a regular basis.*
▶ *Don't give criticism in isolation.*
▶ *Don't use criticism as a first resort.*
▶ *Asking someone how the relevant task is going can turn things into a discussion, or a request for advice or help, instead of criticism being necessary.*
▶ *Be considerate – imagine yourself in the person's shoes.*
▶ *Use open, positive body language, and a warm, supportive voice tone.*
▶ *Remember, everybody makes mistakes and none of us is perfect, even you.*
▶ *Be aware of the circumstances surrounding the person, and take these into account.*

- *Give criticism in private.*
- *Don't wander around the point – come to the point.*
- *Have confidence in what you are saying.*
- *Be absolutely sure of your facts before criticizing someone.*
- *Criticize the behaviour, not the person or their personality.*
- *See the situation as a whole, and keep the criticism in proportion.*
- *If you are angry or upset, wait until you've cooled off before giving criticism.*

Insight

I've lost count of the number of people who tell me they have been criticized harshly by their manager or boss. It seems to me that many managers aren't aware of the above tips, and are damaging their staff's morale because of this.

Anxiety

Tension is often accompanied by worry or anxiety, and this usually disappears with regular use of physical and mental relaxation of any kind. Much of the book so far has addressed this problem. If anxiety is left untreated, or if relaxation has little effect, an 'anxiety disorder' can develop. This can take a variety of forms, and usually requires specialist treatment, which takes what you've learned here further and in more detail, and may also involve the use of medication, which can be very effective. For a better knowledge of this let's look a bit more closely at the anxiety disorders which can be an outcome of long-term anxiety.

PANIC DISORDER

Although an occasional bout of anxiety or a panic attack brought about by stress or some other situation can present little problem to some people, for others these may become frequent and a source of great distress. This condition, now known as anxiety or panic disorder, may even continue when the original stress has been resolved. As already described, an anxiety or panic attack is a period of intense fear or discomfort, usually reaching a peak within ten minutes. It is accompanied by a wide range of symptoms such as palpitations, dizziness, shaking, sweating and a fear of losing control.

Insight

Unpleasant though having panic attacks is, this problem can be treated relatively easily, especially if caught early. So don't hesitate, and get along to your doctor as soon as you can, if you have experienced this.

PHOBIAS

For some people, their anxiety becomes attached to particular situations or objects, and a phobia can develop. The most common life-restricting phobias are agoraphobia and social phobia. And, contrary to popular belief, these phobias are in no way irrational. In most cases, fear of suffering a panic attack or other symptoms in public lies at its heart – not an unreasonable fear. People are not actually afraid of going out; they fear these unpleasant symptoms, or being embarrassed in public. The sufferer feels there is no logical explanation for the panic attack, so the initial attack quickly becomes associated with where it happened, leading to a build-up of avoidance, and further anxiety. The person's nervous system reacts as if it has decided that if no other explanation for the panic attack is forthcoming, it must have been something to do with where they were at the time, or some object or animal which was present at the time.

Agoraphobia

An often underestimated and misunderstood condition, agoraphobia overwhelmingly affects women rather than men, though the reasons for this are not yet clearly understood. This may simply be because women are more likely to admit to it, or perhaps their often home-based lifestyle fosters its development. Often wrongly taken to be fear of open spaces, agoraphobia is in fact a fear of leaving the security of home, particularly if required to go to crowded places, or to wait in a queue of any kind.

Again, it is the symptoms experienced when outside which are feared, not being outside *per se*. Unpleasant symptoms experienced when out of the home become associated with being away from home, and a pattern of avoidance and increased fear can very easily and quickly spiral into a serious and life-restricting fear.

It is not uncommon for professional and business men or women to suffer from agoraphobia, yet still manage to function completely adequately, so long as they have a car to travel around in. For agoraphobics, the car is often a substitute for the security of the home, and they simply take it around with them, wherever they go, like a security blanket.

Social phobia

Again more common than perhaps assumed, social phobia can develop in a similar way to agoraphobia. The main difference is probably that the situation avoided is that of having to 'perform' in some way in front of one or more people. Having to converse, dance, give a talk or demonstration, eat or drink, all may become a source of embarrassment or fear if visible symptoms of anxiety occur. Blushing, sweating, shaking, panicking, stammering, feeling off balance or light-headed, all can be caused by anxiety, and all can encourage avoidance of a range of social situations. The acid test of whether a social phobia is involved is whether the person can perform the required behaviour when alone, and only succumbs to anxiety when other people are present.

Case study – Gary

Gary is a young man who has been under a bit of stress at work. His hand shook a little one day, a few weeks ago, when he was signing for something at the bank. He felt very embarrassed, and avoided having to do so again. Then a week or two later, his hand shook when he was drinking with his friends, so now he avoids outings with his friends in case it happens again and they laugh at him. He is now so scared of his hand shaking, that his fear has made it happen more often, reinforcing the belief that it will happen. He feels that he is going to pieces, and now won't go out anywhere that his shaking hand may be seen by others. He has even begun to avoid eating with his family in case his hand shakes.

So, apparently illogical behaviour has a logical explanation. A similar pattern can explain people who find meeting and talking to others difficult, or who fear speaking, acting or singing in public.

Simple phobias
Simple phobias such as fear of snakes, spiders, birds, dogs, cats and so on are most likely to have been acquired through a fright, or by copying someone else in childhood. There is also some evidence of humans being prepared genetically to fear potentially lethal creatures such as snakes and insects, and dangerous situations such as heights. Fainting at the sight of blood, injury or injections has also been explained as a primitive adaptive response to personal injury, which had the purpose of lowering blood pressure to minimize blood loss and the danger of shock.

Obsessive-compulsive disorder

Many people have their own harmless and quite normal obsessions or compulsions. Many of us simply have to put a pinch of salt over our shoulder after spilling it; will not walk on the lines of the pavement or under a ladder; must have ornaments or books displayed in a certain way; or find ourselves checking twice that the gas is off or the door locked, even though we know we've just checked it. If these various needs are not met, we suffer a pang of anxiety. This is the everyday behaviour on which the anxiety disorder, obsessive-compulsive disorder, or OCD, can gradually be built. It's difficult to estimate how many people have OCD, as many never present for treatment through embarrassment or the constraints of the condition. However, recent studies suggest it to be more common than previously thought, and may approach a rate of two people in every 100 at any time. We are probably all familiar with well-known obsessives such as the recluse Howard Hughes, but there is also likely to be one perhaps less extreme sufferer in an average street.

Linda is 32, and works part-time in a sweet shop near to her home to help make ends meet, as her husband has a very low-paid job. She also cares for her elderly grandmother who suffers from senile dementia, and even though her grandmother goes for day care every day, Linda finds everything just too much, and has felt very tense and anxious for many months.

While her grandmother is at home with her, she has a habit of turning on the gas cooker, and Linda is terrified of a fire or explosion as a result. One day a few months ago, she checked the cooker was off before leaving for work, but as soon as she had locked the front door, she felt anxious in case the gas was still on even though she had just checked it. Might as well make sure, she thought, better safe than sorry. So she returned to check.

The next day she found herself doing the same thing, checking twice, as she felt anxious if she didn't make sure, and there was no harm in checking. This went on for a few weeks, until one day she found herself having to check three times in order to be convinced that the gas really was off, and to reduce her anxiety. Sometimes she would get halfway to work, then have to come back to check.

Now, after several months, she has to allow an extra ten minutes to get ready for work, as she can't relax unless she checks four times that the gas is off before leaving. She knows this is stupid, but she just can't help herself. The anxiety gets so bad if she tries not to do it, that she just can't bear it. She's scared to tell anyone in case they think she's going mad.

Obsessions are intrusive unwanted thoughts, ideas or impulses, which repeatedly recur in a person's mind, sometimes of a frightening nature. Compulsions, sometimes known as rituals, are behaviours repeated to reduce the anxiety caused by the obsessive thought. So, Linda's obsessive thought was of the house blowing up due to a gas explosion, and her compulsion was to check that the gas was off. Likewise, if a person has obsessive thoughts centred on a fear of dirt or germs, then they may compulsively wash and clean themselves and the house to reduce the anxiety caused by the thoughts. Other common obsessive thoughts include repetitive counting, blasphemous thoughts, or vivid images of harming a loved family member. The compulsions most commonly reported to Obsessive Action, a UK self-help charity, include excessive hand-washing, house cleaning, checking of water, gas taps and electric switches.

KEY POINTS

Look back over this chapter and choose the FIVE pieces of information you found to be most interesting or helpful. Write these here, or go back and underline or highlight them in some way.

1 ....

2 ....

3 ....

4 ....

5 ....

Look back over this chapter and choose the FIVE practical suggestions you found to be most useful. Write these here, or go back and underline or highlight them in some way.

1 ....

2 ....

3 ....

4 ....

5 ....

Which FOUR techniques or suggestions from this chapter would you like to work towards using regularly?

Write these here, or go back and underline or highlight them in some way.

1 ....

2 ....

3 ....

4 ....

12

Relaxation in situations

In this chapter you will learn:
- *the dual approach to difficult situations*
- *coping strategies for exams and tests*
- *how to be calmer at interviews and presentations*
- *how to stay relaxed with people in authority*
- *ways that visualization and relaxation can help in any situation.*

This chapter will describe how best to use relaxation in a range of situations which most people find can produce tension and anxiety, sometimes well in advance of the actual event. Interviews, driving tests or other exams, dealing with an authority figure, and making a presentation or speech are covered in detail, but the same general principles can be applied to any situation which can cause tension, e.g. a dentist appointment, or going into hospital for an operation.

As in the previous chapter, the approach will be a dual one. Specific skills will be provided for these situations, which, teamed with the relaxation skills learned so far, will mean they can be approached in a far more confident and relaxed way. Whatever the situation, careful preparation is the key to success.

Insight
I find it really helpful to keep in mind that the human species developed with the main aim of lying around a cave most of the day. But our minds and bodies have been catapulted into

this world of ours, which we weren't really designed for. So it's small wonder that so many of us find situations like those discussed in this chapter difficult to deal with.

Preparing to do anything which might make you tense

Some people sail through life without ever experiencing tension or anxiety. But they are very much in the minority. For most people, there will be circumstances, particular people, places or scenarios, which cause tension or anxiety. And no two people will be exactly the same. A situation which doesn't bother your friend, may produce almost crippling tension for you. And vice versa. This is because we all have different personalities, different skills and preferences, and different previous experiences, all of which contribute to our pattern of tension. But whatever situation it is that is causing tension, here are some suggestions to help prepare for it:

▶ *In the days or even the weeks before the event, use any form of mental and physical relaxation, for at least 10–15 minutes, to reduce your tension and anxiety. The more anxious you are, the more often and longer you should relax in this way.*

▶ *Be prepared with any method of relaxing quickly which works for you, to use on the day.*

▶ *Watch out for 'negative self-talk' in the days or weeks beforehand such as, 'I'm going to make a fool of myself' or, 'I'm useless at this.' This builds your anxiety and increases your self-doubt. Replace such self-talk with positive and realistic thoughts such as, 'If I use relaxation and prepare well, I can do a reasonable job of this' or, 'I have useful ideas to pass on and using my new skills, I can manage fairly well with this', or 'I'm quite good at this, and with good preparation I can cope.'*

▶ *Use 'visualization'. This has a very powerful and unexpectedly positive effect on tension and anxiety, and also on how things go on the day. It's as if facing up to it all in your mind before an event or situation takes the sting out of the anxiety you feel beforehand, and makes it all very familiar when the day arrives. On the day, it's as if you've 'been there and done that' many times already, but in a relaxed way, so it produces much less tension. You are also much less likely to be tense the next time you have to do something similar. So, before the event, practise every day, visualizing it.*

Try this – Visualize your event

For simplicity, let's call whatever it is you're planning to do an 'event'.

Stage one:

1 *Relax your body and mind using a method which suits you.*
2 *Then, close your eyes and visualize the entire event as clearly as you can. Visualize everything you can, from getting ready, to how you'll get there, to what happens during and after the event, and so on. Visualize everything going well. Spend about 10–15 minutes on this.*
3 *Key things to remember when visualizing are:*
   ▷ *Visualize everything and everyone in as much detail as you can: colours, smells, sights, sounds, speech and so on.*
   ▷ *Whenever you feel any anxiety associated with what you are visualizing, use a quick method of relaxing to reduce that anxiety; when the anxiety falls, continue with the visualization.*

Stage two:

When you are able to complete the entire visualization as in Stage one, you are ready to start to visualize in a different way.

1 *Firstly, list all of the things which, realistically, may go wrong on the day.*
2 *Now beside each, note down how you would best cope if that happened.*

> **3** *Then take these items from your list, one at a time, and*
> *visualize the thing going wrong, and you dealing with it*
> *calmly and appropriately – use your quick relaxation method*
> *to reduce any anxiety this arouses.*

Insight

In my experience, many people can think visualizing like this
is a bit 'out there' and not for them. But take my word for it,
this can work really well, if you give it a try.

Coping with authority figures

For some people, dealing with authority figures can be particularly
daunting or even intimidating. Complaining in a shop or
restaurant, a meeting with the bank manager or accountant, an
interview for a job or a place on a course, or even going to the
doctor can feel like a challenge. Here are some other ideas, in
addition to those just covered, which may make this kind of thing
easier to deal with in a more relaxed way:

▶ *Remember your rights as a human being. You and the person*
  in authority are both just people.
▶ *Imagine the person or people in authority are in funny*
  costumes, or their underwear, or swimwear, or even naked, or
  on the toilet – this helps to make them seem more human, and
  on a more equal footing with you!
▶ *Don't be afraid to have some notes with you – the person in*
  authority will probably have some, so you can too.
▶ *Be sure of your facts – do a bit of research first if necessary.*
▶ *Know your rights in the particular situation – check them out*
  beforehand.
▶ *Keep a 'good' attitude – pleasant, friendly, warm, assertive.*
▶ *Use a warm, low-pitched, calm voice.*
▶ *Use open and friendly body language and posture.*
▶ *Have a list of your questions ready.*

- Keep to your main points – don't be distracted from them.
- Use assertiveness techniques such as:
  - asking for information
  - being specific
  - repeating a point calmly if you feel it hasn't got across
  - fogging
  - accepting fair criticism
  - responding to unfair criticism
  - being ready to say 'no' if appropriate
  - being open to negotiation and compromise.
- Take a friend or other appropriate person along if you can for support.
- Be prepared to go higher up if necessary.

Those who dream by day are cognizant of many things which escape those who dream only by night.

Edgar Allan Poe, American writer, 1809–49

Interview skills

Interviews make everyone nervous. There is usually so much riding on them and, mostly, you've no idea what you might be asked. Nowadays you often have to come prepared with a short talk or presentation ready to deliver on the day. All of this encourages tension. In the usual dual approach, here are some suggestions to help you in this situation:

- Arrive early, half an hour if you can. This gives time for nerves to settle, allows for unexpected traffic jams or late trains, and a visit to the toilet. You also have time to sit quietly and use a relaxation technique.
- Ask for a glass of water at the start if you feel you may dry up during the interview – or bring this in with you. A dry mouth is a common sign of tension.
- Avoid alcohol or very spicy foods the night before (and on the day!), as these can stay on your breath and give a very bad impression.

▶ *Make sure that what you wear is appropriate for the type of interview, and that you will feel comfortable and won't need to think about what you're wearing during the interview. If it's something new, try it out for an hour or two well in advance to check it doesn't have any unforeseen problems, such as clinging, riding up, creasing badly or being too revealing. Layers are always useful to help you cool down, as tension and stress can make you hot and sweaty.*

▶ *It is better not to have the coffee or the biscuits. Spillages and shaky hands are surprisingly common, and talking and eating at the same time isn't easy.*

▶ *Don't be afraid to have some notes – the interviewer/s will have some, so you can too.*

▶ *Don't fiddle with anything during the interview, e.g. your jewellery, pen, anything in your pocket.*

▶ *Enter the room with an upright but relaxed posture; looking confident, even if you don't feel it; shoulders down and relaxed, head up. Shake hands firmly when introduced, and avoid a weak 'dead-fish' handshake.*

▶ *As before, imagine that the person or people in authority are in their underwear, or nude, or on the toilet – this helps to make them seem more human, and on a more equal footing with you!*

▶ *Interviewers will tend to remember the first and last impressions that you make – so pay particular attention to this at the start and end of your interview.*

▶ *Keep a 'good' attitude – pleasant, friendly, warm, assertive. Avoid making jokes.*

▶ *Make sure to end by thanking the interviewers for seeing you, confirming your interest in the job, and saying why you really want the job. Make this only a sentence or two, and prepare it in advance.*

▶ *Make sure to visit the toilet before the interview, and check your appearance while you're there.*

▶ *Make sure you have eaten sensibly before the interview. Low blood sugar makes it difficult to concentrate.*

▶ *Sit or stand with an open and relaxed posture.*

▶ *The key point for any interview is to* be prepared. *Think through the questions you might be asked, and prepare your answers. Good interviews, like good food, rely on careful and organized preparation.*

▶ *Watch what you are doing before and after the interview, while still on the potential employer's territory, or if you are being shown round by another member of staff. Other staff are often asked for their opinion of you during these times. So stay relaxed and focused, show a real interest, and make relevant, sensible comments.*

Insight

My personal favourite in these situations is to imagine the authority figures dressed as a large white rabbit, with huge floppy ears. I think this is because I really enjoyed watching a 1950 film in which the actor James Stewart's best friend was an invisible six foot high white rabbit called 'Harvey'. What would you choose?

Pointers for exams or tests

Whether it be a school or college exam or a driving test, or a practical exam in hairdressing, tap dancing or in alternative therapy, being overly tense and anxious will detract from your performance. You want to be geared up for what you have to do, but no more. It is a myth that a bit of stress is good for you in these situations. What this really means is you need to be alert and geared up appropriately for what is being asked of you, not laid back, half-asleep and apathetic.

First up, you must believe in yourself. You wouldn't have been given a place on the course, or been put forward for this test or exam, if you didn't have the ability to do it. Therefore, if you prepare properly, things should go well. Don't try to be perfect. It's great to succeed and reach for the stars. But keep things in balance. If you think that 'anything less than A+ means I've failed' then you are creating mountains of unnecessary stress for yourself. Aim to do your best, but recognize that none of us can be perfect all of the time.

Take steps to overcome problems as soon as they arise. If you find you don't understand some of your course material, or don't know how to prepare for the exam, getting stressed out won't help. Instead, take action to address the problem directly by seeing your course tutor or getting help from your classmates, straight away. Don't keep things bottled up. Confiding in someone you trust and who will be supportive is a great way of alleviating tension. Keep things in perspective. The exam might seem like the most crucial thing right now, but in the grander scheme of your whole life it is only a small part. And you can always take it again.

Tips for the revision or preparation period:

▶ *Leave plenty of time to revise or prepare, so that you don't get into a situation of having to do last-minute cramming or practice. This approach will help to boost your confidence and reduce any pre-exam tension, as you will know you have prepared well.*
▶ *Develop a timetable so that you can track and monitor your progress. Make sure you allow time for fun and relaxation so that you avoid burning out.*
▶ *When you are revising, as soon as you notice your mind is losing concentration, take a short break. You will then come back to your revision refreshed.*
▶ *Experiment with several alternative revision techniques so that revision is more fun and your motivation to study is high.*
▶ *Don't drink too much coffee, tea or fizzy drinks, the caffeine will 'hype' you and make your thinking less clear. Eat healthily and regularly, your brain will benefit from the nutrients.*
▶ *Regular moderate exercise will boost your energy, clear your mind and help you to relax.*
▶ *Use relaxation techniques every day, several times a day for a few minutes if possible. They will help to keep you feeling*

calm and balanced, improve your concentration levels and help you to sleep better.

Tips for the exam itself:

▸ *Plan to get there early. But don't take part in 'worry and panic chat' with other students.*
▸ *Ensure you have all the necessary equipment.*
▸ *Take a deep breath, then let it out slowly as you relax your shoulders and arms, before you start to read the paper.*
▸ *Read through the paper before you decide which questions to answer.*
▸ *Work out the time allocation for each question, and stick to it.*
▸ *Start with an answer you are confident about.*
▸ *If you feel yourself panicking, take a slow deep breath in, then sigh it out slowly, allowing your shoulders to relax, then use a relaxation technique to relax further.*
▸ *Don't spend endless time afterwards criticizing yourself for where you think you went wrong. Often our own self-assessment is far too harsh. Congratulate yourself on the things you did right, learn from the bits where you know you could have done better, and then move on.*

Insight

If you are acutely anxious about an exam, and begin worrying months ahead, you are not alone. In such cases, I've found it's best to begin to deal with this straight away. Talk to someone in charge of things, as there is often special support available, or begin using all the ideas in this book right from the start – don't wait until a few days or weeks before the exam or test. Give yourself time.

Giving a presentation, speech or short talk

A bit of tension and anxiety immediately before having to speak in public is normal and to be expected, but if it is particularly acute or lasts more than a few hours, it is helpful to try to do something about it. Some people feel anxious some days or even weeks before having to give a talk.

Public speaking doesn't need to be a formal talk to a large audience. It can be giving a report at work to your team, or reading a story to a group of five-year-olds. Even speaking to a group of two or three people can make people feel nervous. Getting used to the sound of your own voice can really help with this. Sometimes the sound of your own voice can be the most frightening thing in the world, if you're not used to it. So sing in the shower, shout in the bath, talk to the dog, give yourself a pep talk in the mirror, anything which gets you more familiar with being the only one that's talking or making a noise! This can be especially relevant to anyone brought up in the 'children should be seen and not heard' era.

As before, here are some more suggestions to help make this kind of thing easier. Many of these ideas refer to a formal talk, so if this is not currently of interest to you, and you are more interested in speaking to a small group, just focus on the suggestions which might be useful to you now. But remember that this information is here, as you never know when you might need it!

If you have time, it is best to build up these skills gradually, building confidence as you go. So start with something small, and practise this until you're confident with it, then take things up a stage, practise at that level until you're feeling good with it, then move up to the next stage and so on.

Here are some more ideas:

▶ *Be ready to use a method of relaxing quickly, when you are waiting to start your presentation, and at any time during the event when you feel anxious.*
▶ *Make sure you have prepared your talk or presentation well, and have any visual or other aids you might need ready.*
▶ *Do some practice runs through, but not too many as you will become over-familiar with it.*

► *Get there in good time, so that you can find the room, check that any required equipment is there, set the chairs out the way you want them, and get everything organized to make things go smoothly.*

► *Never begin by telling your audience that you're not very good at public speaking, or that you're nervous. This reduces your authority straight away, and makes your audience lack confidence in you. Their body language will reflect this and you'll pick this up and interpret this as lack of interest or confirmation of a poor performance, making you more anxious and more likely to perform less well – a self-fulfilling prophecy!*

► *Finally, remember that you only have to do a fair and reasonable job on this – you don't need to be stunning, outstanding, and give the best talk they've ever had – achieving that would just be a bonus, and will come with practice.*

Insight

I've often heard people being advised to focus on an object right at the back of the room, or on one friendly looking member of the audience, when giving a talk. Think how your audience will feel if you stare straight past them, or keep looking at just one (very embarrassed) person. No, it's much better to let your eyes move continuously and smoothly around your whole audience.

KEY POINTS

Look back over this chapter and choose the FIVE pieces of information you found to be most interesting or helpful. Write these here, or go back and underline or highlight them in some way.

1 ....

2 ....

3 ....

4 ....

5 ....

Look back over this chapter and choose the FIVE practical suggestions you found to be most useful. Write these here, or go back and underline or highlight them in some way.

1 ....

2 ....

3 ....

4 ....

5 ....

Which FOUR techniques or suggestions from this chapter would you like to work towards using regularly?

(Contd)

Write these here, or go back and underline or highlight them in some way.

1 ....

2 ....

3 ....

4 ....

13

Relaxation and your mood

In this chapter you will learn:
- *some causes of mood swings and moodiness*
- *how relaxation can help you to cope better with moodiness or premenstrual symptoms*
- *lots of tips for raising your mood, if it is 'down'*
- *about depression.*

This is the third of three chapters which will show you how to deal with specific situations, using the dual approach of relaxation along with a better understanding. This chapter will concentrate on a problem which everyone has experienced from one side or the other, moodiness.

If you are prone to tension and anxiety, you may well be more vulnerable to moodiness and mood swings too. Things that others might not even notice can be upsetting, leaving you tense, worried, angry or in tears. You may be very touchy, with a tendency to overreact, become jealous, or take offence. Arguments and upsets may be common.

Everything in this book should help you to become more relaxed, less tense, and more at ease with yourself. All of this will reduce moodiness. This chapter will take this a little further, and look at things from a different perspective, by focusing on the mood swings themselves, and by explaining many possible ways to lessen these and smooth things out for you.

Here are just some of the problems being moody can cause:

- *worry*
- *anxiety*
- *tearfulness*
- *up one minute, down the next*
- *longer downs*
- *increased tension*
- *constant rows and arguments*
- *anger and frustration*
- *depression*
- *guilt*
- *feeling that nobody understands*
- *introversion*
- *cutting yourself off*
- *sudden mood swings*
- *never knowing where you are*
- *self-loathing*
- *anger and aggression*
- *sudden outbursts*
- *regret*
- *violence*
- *damage to property*
- *damage to relationships*
- *difficulties keeping a relationship going.*

Reasons for mood problems

But what causes moodiness? Could there be more to it than just
another symptom of being anxious, stressed or tense? Let's look
at some other possible reasons for moods, and mood swings.
Some affect only women, but some apply to men too. They are all

relevant to everyone really, because you can be just as tense, if not more so, if you are at the other side of someone who is in a mood. Of course, any or all of these causes of moodiness can be affecting you over and above your being tense or anxious, giving a sort of doubling or even trebling of the effect. So it's well worth learning how to do something about these too.

> **Insight**
>
> It's a great idea to plan ahead, but I sometimes find if I'm not sure where I'm headed and I'm tired and drained, just taking a first step, just any one which seems reasonable at the time, will get me started, and get me moving and on my way. The next step seems to simply fall into place itself after that, without any soul searching.

MID-LIFE CRISES (WOMEN AND MEN)

Many of us find that when we reach our late thirties or early forties, we begin to question what life is all about, and where we are going. You can become acutely aware of ambitions unrealized, and that others are doing much better than you are in the race that is today's life. What have you achieved so far? Is it too late to achieve anything else? What's the point of it all? You may lose your parents or your partner and suddenly feel there is nothing standing between you and the end of your life. This can leave you feeling scared, vulnerable and lost for a while. Don't be afraid to talk these feelings out with a trusted friend or adviser. A life coach or counsellor can also be very helpful in these circumstances.

BLOOD SUGAR LEVELS (MEN AND WOMEN)

One of the main reasons people get angry seemingly out of the blue is because their blood sugar level is low. Low blood sugar makes you feel you want to eat something sweet, and it can also make you more likely to feel angry. As already described in an earlier chapter, to avoid highs and lows of your blood sugar, you should eat small and healthy regular meals, and avoid refined sugar products. Have a healthy snack between meals too. So don't skip breakfast and then fill up on a doughnut or muffin for elevenses. This will just give you a high, followed by a sudden dip, and that's the danger time for a low mood.

The next three sections will deal with periods, childbirth and the menopause. You can skip these if you prefer and go straight to 'What you can do to help yourself'.

BEFORE A PERIOD

Don't listen to any of those media and expert reports which say that pre-menstrual syndrome (PMS) doesn't exist. It does. And it can have a very powerful effect on mood. There can be hyperactivity, low mood, sudden mood swings, outbursts of anger, all along with quite irrational thinking. Many an argument happens at this time of the month. My husband will vouch for that, and the irrational thinking. There is much you can do to help yourself, mainly staying fit and eating a healthy balanced diet, because certain key vitamins and your blood sugar levels seem to have a major impact on PMS.

Try this – The Food for Mood project

The 'Food for Mood' project, organized by the charity MIND, suggests some ideas on diet to think about and try for yourself to relieve PMS – they are in order of importance:

▶ *Vitamin B$_6$, vitamin C, folic acid (folate) and zinc are all essential good-mood nutrients, and can help with PMS. They are needed to make the feel-good brain chemical serotonin from the tryptophan protein fragment that is found in foods such as meat, fish, beans and lentils. Alternatively, take a good vitamin and mineral supplement every day, or one specially designed for PMS. Good chemists stock a range of these.*
▶ *Evening primrose oil can help with PMS.*
▶ *Watch your blood sugar level. You can avoid the highs and lows of mood and energy associated with fluctuating*

> *blood sugar levels by choosing foods that are digested slowly. So avoid anything containing refined sugar, and go for fresh or dried fruit, nuts, oats, wholewheat cereals etc.*
>
> ▶ *Eating little and often, with no long gaps, also helps keep blood sugar levels constant. So no gaps longer than two or three hours.*
>
> ▶ *Avoid caffeine, as too much can produce nervousness and aggravate pre-menstrual syndrome (PMS).*
>
> ▶ *Very low-fat diets can make you depressed or make PMS more likely. Research has linked diets that drastically cut down on all types of fat with an increase in symptoms of depression and PMS.*
>
> ▶ *Turkey and chicken contain a good source of mood enhancing tryptophan, an essential amino acid which is converted into serotonin – which can be low in people suffering from PMS.*

Speak to your doctor if self-help strategies don't seem to be working. All doctors understand PMS nowadays. It helps if you keep a diary of your behaviour, moods and other symptoms such as bloating, breast tenderness and cravings, for a few months before you attend your doctor. The doctor will be able to help, possibly using medication if your symptoms are particularly severe.

AFTER A BABY

Similarly, after giving birth, the hormones can be all over the place, and will take some time to settle back to normal after the upheaval of pregnancy and breastfeeding. You'll also be even more tired than usual, unless you are very lucky! This can all mean that your moods are volatile, with tears never very far away. In some cases, this may be caused by post-natal depression, so if your mood is consistently very low after your baby is born, have a word with your midwife, health visitor or GP, who should be able to help you. Later in this chapter, there is more guidance on dealing with depression.

Yes, those hormones once again. The several or more years running up to the menopause, when periods actually stop, is called the 'peri-menopause', and during this time, you can be subject to mood swings. You can also find that PMS can become more severe during this time in your life, or you may experience it when you've never been troubled by it before. Periods which are heavier than normal, or irregular and unpredictable, can also leave you feeling on edge, upset and moody. As before, if this is getting too difficult to cope with, rest assured you are not alone, and that your GP should be able to help. If you find it easier to talk about these things with a woman, make an appointment with a female doctor at your practice.

What you can do to help yourself

So, what to do about all these moods and related problems? Is there anything you can do? Yes, of course there is. But you have to work at it. You'll also have to be able to draw yourself up when you're in a mood, and do something different from what the mood is telling you to do! Sometimes, that's much easier said than done. So here are some coping strategies to help you and those around you to deal better with your moods, whatever their cause.

Insight

I know many people who find it helps to set aside 20 minutes or so each day to think about what they're going to do to make things better, rather than thinking about it off and on during each day.

UNDERSTANDING YOUR MOODS BETTER

Somehow just understanding better why you are feeling the way you do can have an amazingly calming effect on your mood. It can give you a kind of release. It can let you off the hook of your own self-imposed guilt. It can also help if your friends, colleagues and partner can understand things better too. So, explain it to them on a good day, or perhaps let them read this chapter.

EXERCISE

Once again, exercise is a factor. Regular exercise will help you to even out those mood swings. It can also help you to feel generally better within yourself, not just physically, because the particular brain physiology which exercise produces makes you feel good. It can also help you to work off feelings of frustration, anger and tension safely. The secret is to choose a form of exercise which you actually enjoy, and which fits easily into your life, as you are much more likely to keep it up.

Insight

My particular 'fix' when it comes to exercise is dancing. Any kind. I've tried a few different types – disco dancing, line dancing, Scottish country dancing, tap dancing. Just choose an activity which is fun for you, and you will be rewarded with the double bonus of getting fit at the same time as enjoying yourself. What would your choice be?

Coping with depression

People tend nowadays to use the word *depressed* as a sort of throwaway comment: 'I'm feeling really depressed about my car. It's always breaking down', 'This weather is so depressing.' And maybe they are genuinely depressed. But it is much more likely that they are simply a bit fed up, a perfectly reasonable reaction, which we can all experience for an hour or two, or a day or two, from time to time.

But true depression is a much more serious and distressing affair. Your mood can become extremely low, for more days than not, over weeks or months. This can vary from occasionally feeling down, to a deeper and more long-lasting experience of feeling very low, weepy and despairing. This is true depression, and is a much more disabling experience, lasting much longer than just a few days. Low mood is likely to be present most days, with long tearful episodes common. Other signs are persistent feelings of hopelessness, despair and anxiety, lack of energy, poor appetite and difficulty sleeping, especially wakening early in the morning. The first and most important thing you should do if you think you might be depressed, is to go along and a have a chat with your doctor.

Research, evidence and statistics

The most common form of mental distress in Britain is mixed anxiety and depression, experienced by 9.2 per cent of adults in Britain. This is followed by general anxiety at 4.7 per cent. These figures show an increase (from 1993 to 2000) in the prevalence of mixed anxiety with depression of 1.4 per cent.

Office for National Statistics, 2000

Sometimes this kind of depression is simply caused by a chemical imbalance in the body, which can happen for any number of reasons. But sometimes it is the outcome of long-term and difficult life experiences. So tension, anxiety or stress, which has gone on for a long time, can sometimes make a person feel clinically depressed. This is by no means always the outcome, but it can happen.

Dealing with low mood

Whether a down mood is part of a true depression or just a passing experience, it doesn't have to be endured until it lifts. Here are some suggestions, firstly for preventing its occurrence in the first place, and secondly for lifting it should it appear. Catching it early is always a good strategy. Do something about it the minute you recognize its approach or presence.

Tips for *preventing* 'low mood':

- *Relax often.*
- *Have fun regularly.*
- *Keep stress, tension and their effects to a minimum.*
- *Be nice to yourself.*
- *Eat healthily and regularly: little and often is best.*
- *Don't blame yourself.*
- *Don't dwell on working out what has caused your mood.*
- *Keep busy.*
- *Explain to your partner, and anyone else who needs to know, so they understand. Explain to them how they can help you when you are down.*
- *Exercise regularly.*
- *Watch that your diet isn't too low fat, as there is evidence to suggest that eating a diet which is too low in fat can give you a low mood, or even depression.*
- *Smile at people whenever you can.*
- *Always have to hand some activities which will take up your mind for a little while when needed: a magazine to read, calls to friends, Sudoku, a jigsaw or crossword puzzle, mind games, craftwork, whatever you find will take up your thoughts for a while.*
- *Make sure to have quality 'me-time' regularly.*
- *Relax the mind often.*
- *Get into the habit of thinking a positive thought whenever you can. Sounds silly, but this can really help. You may not feel positive at first, but think the thought anyway, and very gradually, with each day, you'll begin to feel a little of the positive feeling that goes with it.*
- *Have more rest and breaks.*
- *Do relaxing things too.*
- *Do lots of enjoyable and rewarding things.*

Tips for *lifting* 'low mood' when it appears:

▶ *Do something active, no matter what it is. Moving around and
doing things helps to lift your mood – housework, gardening,
aerobics, cycling, dancing, walking, and so on.*

▶ *If you can manage to start doing something, anything, the rest
will follow without effort, and you'll feel the benefit.*

▶ *Don't dwell on working out what has caused your low mood.
It will also usually improve by itself as the day goes on.*

▶ *Don't give in to temptation and sit down to brood in that
comfy armchair or sofa.*

▶ *Give a friend a ring and meet for coffee, lunch, a walk,
a talk – anything that will get you out and get your mind
onto something different and more positive.*

▶ *Do something for someone else. This can really help.
Make that call you've been meaning to make to a friend
who's having a rough time, check on an elderly or disabled
neighbour, fill that charity bag that's just about to be
collected.*

▶ *Smiling, or better still laughing, can be a great mood lifter.
So have your favourite comedy DVD always to hand, or one
of those books full of amusing snippets.*

▶ *If you have children around, get out an active and fun game
and play it with them, or read them an exciting story, and do
all the voices and actions.*

▶ *Put on your favourite keep-fit DVD and get moving. Children
can join in too.*

▶ *Plant something, anything – some seeds, herbs or bulbs
in the house, conservatory, window box, or the garden or
greenhouse if you have one. Planting something and watching
it grow can really raise your spirits.*

▶ *Call or visit a friend or relative who is always upbeat and
positive. It definitely rubs off.*

▶ *Think some positive thoughts. Anything will do.*

▶ *Try not to make any major decisions when you are feeling depressed. It's difficult to make good choices when your mood is upset. If these can wait, put them off until you are feeling better.*

▶ *Avoid using alcohol or food to make you feel better. It may give you an immediate lift, but this will only be short term, and you'll feel worse again when it wears off. It is all too easy to get into the habit of using alcohol or food to lessen the effects of a low mood, but this can lead to alcohol or weight problems, which you could do without.*

We act as though comfort and luxury were the chief requirements of life, when all we need to make us really happy is something to be enthusiastic about.

Charles Kingsley, writer, 1819–75

There has been a lot to think about in this chapter, with detailed information and suggestions to absorb. This mirrors the whole book so far, which has included all that is happening in the world of relaxation today, along with what has been happening for as far back as we can be sure. There has been much to choose from, to try for yourself, and much to learn. Learning takes time though. Reading the book isn't going to be all there is to it. Learning needs you to get involved and active in the process too, and then to keep that going. This is a starting point, but you need to take this all forward now. The final chapter will show you some ways of doing this to best suit your needs, so that you get the best from the book now and in the future.

KEY POINTS

Look back over this chapter and choose the FIVE pieces of information you found to be most interesting or helpful. Write these here, or go back and underline or highlight them in some way.

1 ....

2 ....

3 ....

4 ....

5 ....

Look back over this chapter and choose the FIVE practical suggestions you found to be most useful. Write these here, or go back and underline or highlight them in some way.

1 ....

2 ....

3 ....

4 ....

5 ....

Which FOUR techniques or suggestions from this chapter would you like to work towards using regularly?

Write these here, or go back and underline or highlight them in some way.

1 ....

2 ....

3 ....

4 ....

14

What now? Relaxation as a way of life

In this chapter you will learn:
- *how to make relaxation part of your life*
- *to get the most from this book*
- *ways to plan ahead*
- *how to stay motivated.*

Before finishing off this book, it's important to say that this is not the end, but only the beginning for you. Like learning to cook, or to speak a new language, the learning continues, and your skills can develop, diversify and improve for as long as you want them to. You can take this new skill as far as you want. Keep in mind too, that for a skill like relaxation, like many others, regular practice is needed to keep it fresh and in tip-top condition. It's a 'use it or lose it' type of skill.

> *Every day, in every way, I am getting better and better.*
> Émile Coué, French psychologist and pharmacist, 1857–1926

Motivation and persistence

Even though you have spent time reading this book, and thinking about or trying out all that was on offer, there are two factors which can have a dramatic effect on what happens now. The first of these factors is motivation, and the second and related factor is persistence. How keen are you to keep using and practising your new skills? You have to keep your motivation high, and find the space and energy in your life to stay on track. One way of doing that is to remember why you bought this book in the first place. What was it you wanted to get out of learning to relax? Another is that you will begin to feel the benefits of relaxation immediately as you build it in to your life, even in the smallest of ways. And there are so many benefits. There's nothing like success to motivate and encourage you.

The second factor is persistence. Can you persist with the effort needed? What about when the novelty wears off? It is essential to choose techniques which you enjoy, and which fit in easily with your life, and with those around you, so that it becomes a part of your life, not an add-on. This makes it simple to relax regularly, to keep your new skills up to speed, and to keep on learning. No real effort is required. There is always something new happening in the field of relaxation, so there should be new and interesting methods and gadgets to try out, and fresh ideas to think through. This also makes staying with it effortless.

Here are some other ideas which you may find helpful:

▶ *If you can, tell a few trusted people about what you're doing – then they'll ask you about it, and you won't want to show yourself up if you don't stick to it.*
▶ *Out of sight is often out of mind where plans are concerned. So, write down what you plan to do in large, brightly coloured print on a poster-sized sheet of paper, and display it prominently somewhere you can't miss it. For more private or confidential plans, write them on a card and keep them somewhere only you will see them. If you are creative, or good with computer graphics, you can make this much more creative, effective and eye-catching.*
▶ *Recruit a friendly mentor or supporter to encourage you or badger you, whichever works for you! Your mentor can*

also be the person you call on when you are tempted to let things slip.

▶ *For the technologically minded, you could arrange for a 'pop-up' to appear on your PC screen or mobile phone every week, or every day, to remind and encourage you. Something like: 'Remember you were going to use breathing techniques at work this week – go on, you can do it!'*

▶ *Success is more likely if you just have one new thing to do at a time. You are far more likely to stick to just one than if you have a whole list to work on. So if you have got more than one, take them one at a time – one a fortnight or one a month perhaps.*

▶ *You're also much more likely to stick to a plan which is realistic and do-able. So if you've slipped already, maybe you could adapt yours to be easier to actually achieve. Be honest about what you can realistically manage. You can always take the next step after you've managed the first more realistic one, and then the next, and so on. The longest of journeys begins with a single step. So if you've decided to use Total Relaxation every few days, and have already failed miserably, how about aiming for once a week?*

▶ *Write down the benefits you (or someone else) will gain from your plans. Read these regularly, especially when tempted to give up. So instead of sitting feeling tense, read through your list of the benefits of relaxation, and motivate yourself to put down the coffee and the newspaper and do some t'ai chi.*

▶ *Set yourself actual targets, rather than having vague resolutions. So, perhaps aim to do a long relaxation session every Saturday morning, and a five-minute one on Monday and Thursday evenings, instead of constantly looking out for 'a window' to appear in your schedule. Much easier to actually achieve, and you'll know you've done it too, and feel good about it. You can always change it to suit.*

Yesterday is but today's memory, tomorrow is today's dream.

Kahil Gibran, Lebanese artist and poet, 1883–1931

Visualization

This has already been covered, as a way of preparing to do anything which might make you tense or anxious. But you can use visualization in many ways. One is as a form of encouragement and motivation. For instance, you can use it to let you experience what relaxation can do for your everyday life. This can be extremely motivational, especially if repeated on a regular basis.

Try this – Calming visualization

1 *Relax your mind and body thoroughly using any one of your favourite techniques.*
2 *Then, as clearly as you can, visualize yourself as a totally relaxed person, completely at ease, and with lots of self-esteem, working your way through part of an average day. Perhaps start with getting up in the morning, or arriving at work, or going out for the evening.*
3 *Do everything you usually do, and be relaxed, calm and totally at ease.*
4 *Visualize yourself as clearly as you can: see yourself and others, see the colours, hear what's going on, feel the sensations, walk around if it makes it seem more real for you, speak out loud the words you would say. Deal with your day calmly and confidently. Hear what is said to you.*
5 *Experience everything that happens as clearly and in as much detail as you can.*
6 *Take time to think if any problems arise, and visualize how you can deal with things calmly, and without a fuss.*
7 *Feel the satisfaction.*
8 *Notice how calm your breathing is.*
9 *Enjoy the feeling of relaxation and the complete absence of unnecessary tension.*
10 *Spend between five and ten minutes visualizing in this way, before slowly rousing.*

The big picture

You've now almost reached the end of this book. It's good that you're come this far, and are still working hard on all these activities.

Much has been covered, and there is lots more for you to do over the next few weeks and months. As you've progressed through the book, or dipped in to it, you've spent time on various styles of relaxation, for mind and body, and for both. You've also learned breathing and thinking techniques, assertiveness, visualization, guided imagery, and so on. So it's useful at this stage to try to pull all of this together, to review what you've learned, and pick out what has been most important and relevant for you. In other words, it's time to look at the 'bigger picture'. I've always found this helps to consolidate what I've learned, and makes it easier to remember too.

So, flicking back through this book as required, and refreshing your memory of chapter key points, go on and complete your 'big picture' on the next page.

YOUR BIG PICTURE

Here is a template for your Big Picture, all ready to complete. Look back over this book as necessary, and complete the following as best you can. You can also include page numbers to help you find sections again when you are looking for them.

List here the **three or four main good or positive things** you've learned **about yourself:**
- ▶
- ▶
- ▶
- ▶

Which **three or four methods of relaxing your body** worked best for you?
- ▶
- ▶
- ▶
- ▶

Which **three or four methods of relaxing your mind** worked best for you?
▶
▶
▶
▶

Which **one or two breathing techniques** worked best for you?
▶
▶

List the **three or four main things** you will do to combat stress:
▶
▶
▶
▶

List in the left-hand column any reasons you might be more **vulnerable to stress.**
In the right hand column, say how you might make this **less of a problem.**

In the left-hand column, list some **situations you find make you tense.**
Then in the right-hand column, note the most useful things you've learned about **dealing with this situation.**

List here the **three or four most useful things** you've learned about new technological advances, and/or **the Internet** (if any):
▶
▶
▶
▶

(Contd)

List here the **ten most useful things** you've learned **overall from this book:**

▶

▶

▶

▶

▶

▶

▶

▶

▶

▶

List here the things you will find useful **for helping friends or family:**

▶

▶

▶

▶

Personal action plan

But you're not quite finished! Don't put the pencil or pen down just yet... The final thing we want you to do is to work on your 'Personal Action Plan'. This is an overall plan of action, which brings together everything from the book that you want to take forward.

There is no point in reading a book like this and then quietly closing it, putting it in the bookcase, and thinking how interesting it has all been. No, this is just the start. Take action now. Now and in the next few weeks and months, or however long it needs to take. And look back over the book every so often to keep tabs on some of the main things you've discovered or learned on the way through. Use it as a reference, to dip into when needed.

So now, take whatever time you need, and look back over the book, at your Big Picture, and any chapter key points that you need reminding about. From this, take your time and make up your Personal Action Plan. Instructions and a template for this are given opposite. Take whatever time you need. This can require a bit of thinking!

All that remains to say now is that I hope you've found this a useful book, and found relaxation as helpful as I have over the years. I wish you great success in improving your relaxation skills, moving forward and enjoying your life, and passing on what you've learned to others who are in need of calm and peace.

YOUR PERSONAL ACTION PLAN

Here is a template ready for you to complete. This is a starting point which you can adapt as necessary.

List here the main things you've learned from the book, **and are already using:**
▶
▶
▶
▶
How motivated do you feel to continue to use what you've learned in the book, to become more relaxed?
Who might help you with this?

(Contd)

Looking back over the book, make a list of the **actions or changes (large and small)** you plan **for the next month**, along with when you hope to do this:

ACTION OR CHANGE   WHEN?   PRIORITY

▶

▶

▶

▶

▶

▶

▶

▶

▶

▶

Now go back and give each a priority ranking number, starting with 1 as the most important, and so on.

Looking back over the book, make a **list of the actions or changes (large and small)** you plan **for the next two to three months**, along with when you hope to do this:

ACTION OR CHANGE   WHEN?   PRIORITY

▶

▶

▶

▶

▶

▶

▶

▶

▶

▶

Now go back and give each a priority ranking number, starting with 1 as the most important, and so on.

Looking back over the book, make a list of the **actions or changes (large and small)** you plan **for three months and beyond,** along with when you hope to do this:

ACTION OR CHANGE   WHEN?   PRIORITY

▶

▶

▶

▶

▶

▶

▶

▶

▶

▶

Now go back and give a priority ranking number, starting with 1 as the most important, and so on.

Taking it further

Recommended reading

Back, Ken (2005) *Assertiveness at Work*, McGraw-Hill Publishing.

Charlesworth, Edward A. and Nathan, Ronald G. (2004) *Stress Management, a Comprehensive Guide to Wellness*, Ballantine Books.

Dryden, Windy and Constantinou, Daniel (2004) *Assertiveness Step by Step*, Sheldon Press.

Ellis, Richard (2002) *Reiki and the Seven Chakras: Your Essential Guide to the First Level*, Vermilion.

Geary, Amanda (2001) *The Food and Mood Handbook*, Thorsons.

Gunaratana, Bhante Henepola (2002) *Mindfulness in Plain English*, Wisdom Publications.

Harrison, Eric (1994) *Teach Yourself to Meditate: Over 20 Exercises for Peace, Health and Clarity of Mind*, Piatkus Books.

Lindenfield, Gael (2000) *Managing Anger: Simple Steps to Dealing with Frustration and Threat*, Thorsons.

Lindenfield, Gael (2000) *Super Confidence: Simple Steps to Build Self-Assurance*, Thorsons.

Looker, Terry and Gregson, Olga (2010) *Manage Your Stress for a Happier Life*, Hodder Education.

Ozaniec, Naomi (2010) *Beat Stress with Meditation*, Hodder Education.

Ready, Romilla and Burton, Kate (2004) *NLP for Dummies*, Wiley.

Saradananda, Swami (2010) *Relax and Unwind with Yoga*, Hodder Education.

Weller, Stella (1999) *The Breath Book: Breathe Away Stress, Anxiety and Fatigue with 20 Easy Breathing Techniques*, Thorsons.

Wilson, Rob and Branch, Rhena (2005) *CBT for Dummies*, Wiley.

Organizations

International Stress Management Association
PO BOX 491
Bradley Stoke
Bristol
BS34 9AH
Tel: 01179 697284
www.isma.org.uk

MIND
15–19 Broadway
London
E15 4BQ
Helpline: 0845 766 0163
www.mind.org.uk

Mind Cymru
3rd Floor
Quebec House
Castlebridge
5–19 Cowbridge Road East
Cardiff
CF11 9AB
Tel: 029 2039 5123

National Association for Pre-menstrual Syndrome
41 Old Road East
Peckham
Kent
TN12 5AP
Tel: 0870 777 2178
www.pms.org.uk

NHS Direct
General advice on health matters.
Tel: 0845 4647

No Panic
Information and support for panic attacks, phobias, obsessions.
93 Brands Farm Way
Randley
Telford
Shropshire
TF3 2JQ
Free helpline 0808 808 0545, every day, 10 a.m.–10 p.m.
ceo@nopanic.org.uk
www.nopanic.org.uk

Relaxation for Living Institute
1 Great Chapel Street
London
W1F 8FA
Tel: 020 7439 4277

Samaritans
24-hour tel: 08457 90 90 90
jo@samaritans.org

Scottish Association for Mental Health
Cumbrae House
15 Carlton Court
Glasgow
G5 9JP
Tel: 0141 568 7000
enquire@samh.org.uk
www.samh.org.uk

Websites

ACUPUNCTURE

www.acupuncture.com
www.relaxationexpert.co.uk/acupuncture.html

ALEXANDER TECHNIQUE

www.alexandertechnique-itm.org

ALTERNATIVE AND COMPLEMENTARY THERAPY LINKS (GENERAL)

Ireland's holistic directory – www.holisto.com

British Holistic Medical Association – www.bhma.org

British General Council of Complementary Medicine – www.bgccm.org.uk

Internet Health Library – www.internethealthlibrary.com

Federation of Holistic Therapists – www.fht.org.uk

Research Council for Complementary Medicine – www.rccm.org.uk

The British Complementary Medicine Association – www.bcma.co.uk

Holistic Heartbeat – www.holisticheartbeat.com

ANGER

BBC – www.bbc.co.uk/health/emotional_health/mental_health/
BUPA – hcd2.bupa.co.uk/fact_sheets/html/managing_anger
Royal Holloway, University of London –
www.rhul.ac.uk/counselling/common-problems/
anger management.html
www.cks.nhs.uk/patient_information_leaflet/anger_
management

Smart motorist – www.smartmotorist.com/rag

BIOFEEDBACK

Website of Biofeedback Foundation of Europe –
www.bfe.org
www.futurehealth.org
www.stresscheck.co.uk
www.holisticonline.com/Biofeedback.htm
www.aleph1.co.uk

BLOGGING

www.technorati.com
www.blogcatalog.com
www.globalvoicesonline.org
www.blogger.com
www.wordpress.com

COGNITIVE BEHAVIOURAL THERAPY (CBT)

www.babcp.com
www.bacp.co.uk

HUMOUR AND HAPPINESS

European Network for Positive Psychology – www.enpp.eu

University of Pennsylvania –
www.authentichappiness.sas.upenn.edu

BBC – news.bbc.co.uk/1/hi/programmes/happiness_formula/
www.siop.org/tip/Current/04warr.aspx
www.worlddatabaseofhappiness.eur.nl

MASSAGE THERAPY

TEC (training courses) – www.itecworld.co.uk

Chakra School Haad Rin –
www.islandwebs.com/thailand/chakra.htm

The Shiatsu Society (UK) – www.shiatsu.org
www.massagetherapy.co.uk

MEDITATION

www.meditationcenter.com
www.meditation-all-you-need.com/sounds.html

MINDFULNESS

The Centre for Mindfulness Research and Practice within
the School of Psychology, University of Wales Bangor –
www.bangor.ac.uk/mindfulness
www.mindfulness.com
www.priory.com/psych/mindfulness.htm

MUSIC

www.kendavismusic.com/html/relaxation_music.html
www.silenciomusic.co.uk/index.htm

NLP

Association of NLP – www.anlp.org
www.new-oceans.co.uk
www.lambentdobrasil.com
www.NLPInfo.com

REFLEXOLOGY

www.reflexology-research.com/

REIKI

www.reiki.org
www.reikiliving.co.uk

RELAXATION

stress.about.com/od/tensiontamers
stress.about.com/od/autogenictraining
health.discovery.com
www.imaginememedia.com
www.natures-desktop.com

STRESS

International Stress Management Association – www.isma.org.uk
Health and Safety Executive (HSE) – www.hse.gov.uk
www.workstress.net
www.workhealth.org

T'AI CHI/QIGONG

Chinese Wushu Research Institute GB –
www.bigsky.uk.net/index1.html
Provides t'ai chi/qigong instructors and advice to various interested
bodies (such as hospitals, colleges and schools)

www.taichifinder.co.uk
www.qigonghealing.co.uk

Index

abdominal breathing, 96–7
ACTH (adrenocorticotropic hormone), 19
ACTs *see* alternative and complementary therapies
acupuncture, 168–9
   an acupuncture session, 170
   scientific approach to, 170
   self-acupressure, 169–70
   websites, 267
adrenalin, 18, 19
affirmations, 141–2
agoraphobia, 221–2
Alexander Technique (AT), 173–5, 267
Alpha waves, 20–1
alternative and complementary therapies (ACTs), 161–2
   acupuncture, 168–70
   Alexander Technique, 173–5
   biofeedback, 12, 171–3, 187–8, 191–3
   Emotional Freedom Technique (EFT), 177–8
   massage, 162–6
   reflexology, 166–7
   reiki, 175–7
   websites, 267–8, 269, 270
anger, 201–2
   coping with own anger, 206–9

coping with someone else's anger, 209–13
   dealing with rising, 202–3
   is a process, 203–5
   triggers, 205–6
   unhelpful beliefs about, 202
   websites, 268
animals, petting, 150–2
ANS (autonomic nervous system), 19, 61
antidepressants, 55
anxiety, 32–3, 220
   obsessions and compulsions, 223–5
   panic attacks, 33–6, 220–1
   phobias, 221–3
   see also tension
'arousal curve', 21–2
asana, 147–8
assertiveness, 44–7
AT (Alexander Technique), 173–5, 267
Ativan, 55
attitudes, 120
   and stress, 43–4, 71
audio material
   from the imagination, 135–6
   making own, 187
   using sounds, 132–5, 188
   via Internet, 189–91, 270
authority figures, coping with, 231–2

autogenic training, *90–3*
automatic thoughts, *128*
autonomic nervous system (ANS), *19, 61*

baby blues, *245*
Bandler, Dr Richard, *152*
battle fatigue, *38*
beat frequency, *134*
Beck, Dr Aaron, *128*
behaviour therapy, *157*
beliefs, irrational, *122–3*
benefits of relaxation, *2–5*
benzodiazepines, *55*
beta blockers, *56*
Beta waves, *20–1*
Big Picture, your, *258–60*
binaural beats, *134*
biofeedback, *12, 171–2*
    cautions, *172*
    devices without computers, *187–8*
    therapy sessions, *172–3*
    using a computer, *191–3*
    websites, *268*
blogs and blogrolls, *195–7, 268*
blood sugar levels and moods, *243–4*
body language, *101–4*
    changing to relaxed, *106–9, 111–14*
    cultural differences, *115*
'brain-training' games, *188–9*
brainwaves, *19–21*
breathing
    tension and over-breathing, *78–82, 82–7*

breathing techniques, *39–40*
    abdominal breathing, *96–7*
    breathing out, *85*
    letting go, *4–5*
    1-2-3 breathing, *40*
    scanning, *82*
    yoga breathing exercises, *148–9*

CBT (cognitive behavioural therapy), *128, 156–8, 269*
chest pains, hyperventilation and, *85*
Cipramil, *55, 55–6*
cognitive behavioural therapy (CBT), *128, 156–8, 269*
cognitive therapy, *156*
colour meditation, *144*
comfort eating, *73*
compulsions, *224–5*
computers
    biofeedback using, *191–3*
    using, *185–6*
    see also Internet
concentration, poor, *84*
control, sense of, *69–70, 127–8*
cortisol, *18–19*
coughs, hyperventilation and, *84–5*
Craig, Gary, *177*
criticism, *215*
    coping with fair, *216–17*
    coping with unfair, *218–19*
    giving, *219–20*
    handling direct, *215–16*
    handling put-downs, *217–18*

culture
    and body language, *115*
    and vulnerability to
      stress, *62*

Delta waves, *20, 21*
depression, *247–8*
diet, *42–3*
    comfort eating, *73*
    Food for Mood, *244–5*
digestion, hyperventilation and,
    86–7
dizziness, hyperventilation and,
    84
Dove, H.W., *134*
drugs, *54–6, 73*

Eddy, T.J., *151*
Ellis, Dr Albert, *122, 125*
Emotional Freedom Technique
    (EFT), *177–8*
emotions
    anger, *201–13*
    anxiety, *220–3*
    dealing with criticism and
      put-downs, *215–19*
    jealously, *213–15*
    moods and moodiness,
      241–51
    obsessions and compulsions,
      223–5
    and tension, *25*
endorphins, *16*
escapism and stress, *75*
exams, coping with, *234–6*
exercise
    and moodiness, *247*
    and stress management, *42*

experiences, stress and
    previous, *71–2*
eyes
    eye contact, *108–9*
    eye movements when
      thinking, *131, 156*

faintness, hyperventilation
    and, *84*
feelings
    anger, *201–13*
    anxiety, *220–3*
    dealing with criticism and
      put downs, *215–19*
    jealousy, *213–15*
    moods and moodiness,
      241–51
    obsessions and compulsions,
      223–5
'fight or flight' response,
    19, 25–6, 33–4, 204
flushing, hyperventilation and,
    86
Food for Mood project, *244–5*
Friedman, Dr Meyer &
    Rosenman, Dr R, *64, 66*

'galvanic skin response' (GSR),
    171–2, 192
gestures, *112*
glasses, light and sound, *188*
Grinder, John, *153*

handshakes, *107–8*
happiness, *179, 269*
hardy personality, *68–70*
Harper, Robert, *125*
head, position of, *111*

headaches, tension, 83
health benefits of relaxation, 5
hormones, 18–19
horse-riding, 151
humour, 178–81, 269
hyperventilation, 78–9, 81–2
    symptoms of, 82–7
hypothalamus, 19

imagery, 135
    guided, 135–6
    making own material,
     187
    via the Internet, 189–91
Internet
    accessing, 185–6
    biofeedback on, 192
    blogs and blogrolls, 195–7
    podcasts, 189–91
    social networking sites,
     193–5
    tips for using, 186
    useful websites, 267–71
interviews, coping with, 232–4
iPods, 187, 189

Jacobson, Dr Edmund, 11
jealousy, 213–15

Kabat-Zinn, Dr John, 145
Kobasa, Suzanne, 68

laudanum, 55
laughter, 178–81
leisure activities, 49
letting go technique, 4–5
life events and stress, 71–2, 72
life, pace of, 24–5

lifestyle changes and stress
    management, 42–3
light and sound glasses, 188
'locus of control' concept, 70
Lum, L.C., 78

mandalas, 141, 142
mantras, 141–2
massage, 162
    DIY relaxation, 164–6
    precautions, 162–3
    websites, 269
    what to expect, 163–4
    in the workplace, 164
medication, 54–6, 73
meditation, 140–1
    colour meditation, 144–5
    exercises, 142–3
    length of session, 144–5
    mantras and mandalas,
     141–2
    mini-meditations, 143–4
    websites, 269
Meichenbaum, Prof Donald,
    125–6
memory, poor, 84
menopause, 246
mental relaxation methods, 40,
    117–20
    cognitive behavioural
     therapy (CBT), 128, 156–8
    meditation, 140–5
    mindfulness, 145–7
    neurolinguistic
     programming (NLP),
     153–6
    petting an animal, 150–2
    qigong, 152–3

mental relaxation methods (Contd)
t'ai chi, 149–50
using sounds and imagery, 132–6
yoga, 147–9
mid-life crises, 243
mind
changing style of thinking, 43–4
movements when thinking, 131
positive thinking, 125–7
sense of control, 69–70, 127–8
thinking errors, 128–30
mindfulness, 145–7, 269
mini-meditations, 143–4
moods and moodiness, 241
coping with depression, 247–8
help yourself, 246–7
preventing and lifting low mood, 248–51
problems caused by moodiness, 242
reasons for mood problems, 242–6
motivation, 255–6
mouth movements when thinking, 131
MP3 players, 187, 189
muscles
hyperventilation and, 83
tension levels and, 21–3
music, 133–4, 270

neurolinguistic programming (NLP), 153–6, 270

obsessionality, 67–8
obsessive-compulsive disorder (OCD), 223–5
oesophageal dysfunction, 86
1-2-3 breathing, 40
over-activity, 74

pain, hyperventilation and, 83
palpitations, 85
panic attacks, 33–4, 220–1
coping with, 35–6
Partial Relaxation, 104–6
PAUSE routine, 36
perfectionists and stress, 62
persistence and motivation, 255–6
personal action plan, 260–3
personal space, 112–13
personality, 63–4
hardy, 68–70
obsessional, 67–8
Type A and Type B, 64–7
pet therapy, 150–2
phobias, 221–3
pituitary gland, 19
podcasts, 189–91
post-natal depression, 245
post-traumatic stress disorder (PTSD), 38–9
posture, 106–7
Pranayama, 148–9
pre-menstrual syndrome (PMS), 244–5
presentations, giving, 236–8
priorities, sorting out, 47–9
progressive relaxation, 11, 88
Prozac, 55, 55–6

public speaking, *236–8*
put-downs, handling, *217–18*

Qi, *168–9*
qigong, *152–3, 271*
quick relaxation exercises, *91–3*

Rational Emotive Therapy
  (RET), *125*
reflexology, *166–7, 270*
reiki, *175–7, 270*
relationships, benefits of
  relaxation and, *4–5*
relaxation
    aids to, *97–8*
    benefits of, *2–5, 11*
    difficulties relaxing, *9–10*
    dual approach, *200–1, 228*
    explained, *16–18*
    in the past, *1–2*
    uses of, *5–6*
    as a way of life, *254–63*
    websites, *270*
relaxation techniques, *7, 11–12*
    acupuncture, *168–70*
    Alexander Technique,
      173–5
    autogenic training, *90–3*
    biofeedback, *12, 171–3,
      187–8, 191–3*
    cautions, *7–8, 87–8*
    cognitive behavioural
      therapy (CBT), *128,
      156–8*
    and criticism, *216–17,
      218–19, 219–20*
    Emotional Freedom
      Technique (EFT), *177–8*
    frequency of use, *12–13*

gradual change and, *13*
humour and smiling,
  178–81
massage, *162–6*
meditation, *140–5*
mental exercises, *118–20*
mindfulness, *145–7*
neurolinguistic
  programming (NLP),
  153–6
for panic attacks, *35–6*
Partial Relaxation, *104–6*
petting an animal, *150–2*
qigong, *152–3*
reflexology, *166–7*
reiki, *175–7*
slow down technique, *9*
and stress management,
  39–43
t'ai chi, *149–50*
to cope with anger, *208–9*
to cope with jealousy,
  213–14
Total Relaxation, *88–90*
using sound and imagery,
  132–6
visualization, *156, 229–31,
  257*
yoga, *147–9*
resilience, concept of, *69*
RET (Rational Emotive
  Therapy), *125*
revision for exams, *235–6*
Rotter, J.B., *70*
routines, *49–51*

self-speech, *125–6*
serotonin, *42, 96*
Seroxat, *55*

shell shock, *38*
sleep, *93–4*
    tips for a good rest, *94–7*
smiling, *178–81*
social networking sites (SNSs), *193–5*
social phobia, *222–3*
social support, *52, 62*
sounds
    guided, *135–6*
    making own material, *187*
    using, *132–5, 188*
    via the Internet, *189–91, 270*
speeches, giving, *236–8*
SSRIs (selective serotonin re-uptake inhibitors), *55*
stress
    and anxiety, *32–3*
    defining, *27*
    from 'good events', *29*
    historically and today, *30–2*
    is normal, *29*
    signs of, *27–9, 81*
    source of tension, *25–6*
    the stress response, *18–19*
    vulnerability to, *59–72*
    websites, *270*
    see also tension
stress dots and stress cards, *97, 98*
stress management, *38–9*
    attitude change, *43–7*
    exercise and lifestyle, *42–3*
    medication, *54–6*
    relaxation techniques and, *39–40*

social support, *52*
sorting out priorities, *47–9*
time management, *41*
unhelpful coping strategies, *72–5*
using routines, *49–51*
work stress, *52–4*

t'ai chi, *149–50, 271*
talks, giving, *236–8*
tension
    body language and, *101–4, 106–9, 112*
    causes of, *24–6*
    irrational beliefs and, *122–5*
    letting go, *4–5*
    levels of, *21–3*
    physical changes accompanying, *77–8, 78–82, 82–7*
    preparation for possibility of, *229–31*
    vulnerability to, *59–72*
    see also stress; stress management
tests and exams, coping with, *234–6*
Theta waves, *20, 21*
thinking, *40*
    changing style of, *43–4, 120–5*
    errors, *128–30*
    eye, mouth and tongue movements while, *131*
    positive, *125–7*
    see also mind

time management, *41*
tongue movements when
  thinking, *131*
Total Relaxation, *88–90*
touch and touching, *111*
toys, tactile, *97–8*
Type A and Type B
  personalities, *64–7*

Valium, *55*
visual aids
    guided imagery, *135–6*
    making own, *187*
    via the Internet, *189–91*

visualization, *156, 229–31, 257*
voice, tone of, *109–11*

websites
    biofeedback, *192*
    podcasts from, *190*
    social networking, *193–5*
    useful, *267–71*
work, stress caused by, *52–4,
  73–4*

yawning, hyperventilation
  and, *85*
yoga, *147–9*

Image credits

Notes

Notes

Notes